SAXON
MATH

Power Up Workbook

Grade 4

Stephen Hake

Dear Student,

We enjoy watching the adventures of "Super Heroes" because they have power and they use their powers for good. Power is the ability to get things done. We acquire power through concentrated effort and practice. We build powerful bodies with vigorous exercise and healthy living. We develop powerful minds by learning and using skills that help us understand the world around us and solve problems that come our way.

We can build our mathematical power several ways. We can use our memory to store and instantly recall frequently used information. We can improve our ability to solve many kinds of problems mentally without using pencil and paper or a calculator. We can also expand the range of strategies we use to approach and solve new problems.

The Power Up section of each lesson in *Saxon Math 4* is designed to build your mathematical power. Each Power Up has three parts, Facts Practice, Mental Math, and Problem Solving. The three parts are printed on every Power Up page where you will record your answers. This workbook contains a Power Up page for every lesson.

Facts Practice is like a race—write the answers as fast as you can without making mistakes. If the information in the Fact Practice is new to you, take time to study the information so that you can recall the facts quickly and can complete the exercise faster next time.

Mental Math is the ability to work with numbers in your head. This skill greatly improves with practice. Each lesson includes several mental math problems. Your teacher will read these to you or ask you to read them in your book. Do your best to find the answer to each problem without using pencil and paper, except to record your answers. Strong mental math ability will help you throughout your life.

Problem Solving is like a puzzle. You need to figure out how to solve the puzzle. There are many different strategies you can use to solve problems. There are also some questions you can ask yourself to better understand a problem and come up with a plan to solve it. Your teacher will guide you through the problem each day. Becoming a good problem solver is a superior skill that is highly rewarded.

The Power Ups will help you excel at math and acquire math power that will serve you well for the rest of you life.

Stephen Hake

Temple City, California

Estimado estudiante,

Disfrutamos las aventuras de los "Superhéroes" porque tienen poderes y los usan para hacer el bien. Poder es la habilidad de hacer cosas. Adquirimos poder a través de esfuerzo y práctica. Construimos cuerpos fuertes con ejercicio vigoroso y una vida sana. Desarrollamos mentes poderosas aprendiendo y usando habilidades que nos ayudan a entender el mundo a nuestro alrededor y resolviendo los problemas que se nos presentan en el camino.

Podemos construir nuestro poder matemático de diferentes maneras. Podemos utilizar nuestra memoria para almacenar e instantáneamente recordar información de uso frecuente. Podemos mejorar nuestra habilidad para resolver muchos tipos de problemas mentalmente sin usar lápiz y papel o calculadora. También podemos expandir la gama de estrategias que utilizamos para abordar y resolver nuevos problemas.

La sección de Preliminares de cada lección del *Matemáticas intermedias* **Saxon 4** está diseñada para desarrollar tu poder matemático. Cada sección de los Preliminares consta de tres partes, Práctica de operaciones, Cálculo mental y Resolución de problemas. Las tres partes están impresas en cada página de los Preliminares donde registrarás tus respuestas. Este cuaderno de trabajo contiene una página de Preliminares para cada lección.

La Práctica de operaciones es como una carrera—escribe las respuestas tan rápido como puedas sin cometer errores. Si la información en la Práctica de operaciones es nueva para tí, toma el tiempo para estudiar la información para que puedas recordar los problemas con rapidez y completes el ejercicio con mayor rapidez la próxima vez.

El Cálculo mental es la habilidad de trabajar con números mentalmente. La habilidad aumenta enormemente con la práctica. Cada lección incluye varios problemas de cálculo mental. Tu maestro te los leerá o te pedirá que los leas en tu libro. Haz tu mejor esfuerzo para encontrar la respuesta sin usar lápiz y papel, excepto para apuntar tus respuestas. La habilidad de cálculo mental te ayudará por el resto de tu vida.

La Resolución de problemas es como un rompecabezas. Necesitas descubrir cómo resolver el rompecabezas. Existen muchas estrategias distintas que puedes usar para resolver problemas. También existen preguntas que te puedes formular a ti mismo para tener una mejor comprensión de un problema y desarrollar un plan para resolverlo. Tu maestro te guiará a través del problema diariamente. Convertirse en una persona con gran habilidad para resolver problemas te provee de una destreza superior que es enormemente recompensada.

Los Preliminares te ayudarán a destacar en matemáticas y a adquirir poder matemático que te servirá por el resto de tu vida.

Stephen Hake

Temple City, California

Power Up Workbook

Facts   Add.

6 +6	3 +8	5 +9	2 +3	4 +9	3 +4	8 +9	2 +7	0 +3	4 +4
4 +8	2 +9	7 +8	4 +5	9 +1	2 +6	5 +5	6 +7	3 +7	9 +9
7 +9	2 +4	6 +5	3 +3	6 +9	4 +7	0 +0	2 +2	3 +9	5 +8
3 +6	8 +8	4 +6	2 +5	6 +8	3 +5	5 +7	10 +10	2 +8	7 +7

Mental Math

a.	b.	c.	d.
e.	f.	g.	h.

Problem Solving

Understand
What information am I given?
What am I asked to find or do?

- -

Plan
How can I use the information I am given?
Which strategy should I try?

- -

Solve
Did I follow the plan?
Did I show my work?
Did I write the answer?

- -

Check
Did I use the correct information?
Did I do what was asked?
Is my answer reasonable?

Facts   Add.

6 +6	3 +8	5 +9	2 +3	4 +9	3 +4	8 +9	2 +7	0 +3	4 +4
4 +8	2 +9	7 +8	4 +5	9 +1	2 +6	5 +5	6 +7	3 +7	9 +9
7 +9	2 +4	6 +5	3 +3	6 +9	4 +7	0 +0	2 +2	3 +9	5 +8
3 +6	8 +8	4 +6	2 +5	6 +8	3 +5	5 +7	10 +10	2 +8	7 +7

Mental Math

a.	b.	c.	d.
e.	f.	g.	h.

Problem Solving

Understand
What information am I given?
What am I asked to find or do?

- -

Plan
How can I use the information I am given?
Which strategy should I try?

- -

Solve
Did I follow the plan?
Did I show my work?
Did I write the answer?

- -

Check
Did I use the correct information?
Did I do what was asked?
Is my answer reasonable?

Facts   Add.

6 + 6	3 + 8	5 + 9	2 + 3	4 + 9	3 + 4	8 + 9	2 + 7	0 + 3	4 + 4
4 + 8	2 + 9	7 + 8	4 + 5	9 + 1	2 + 6	5 + 5	6 + 7	3 + 7	9 + 9
7 + 9	2 + 4	6 + 5	3 + 3	6 + 9	4 + 7	0 + 0	2 + 2	3 + 9	5 + 8
3 + 6	8 + 8	4 + 6	2 + 5	6 + 8	3 + 5	5 + 7	10 + 10	2 + 8	7 + 7

Mental Math

a.	**b.**	**c.**	**d.**
e.	**f.**	**g.**	**h.**

Problem Solving

Understand
What information am I given?
What am I asked to find or do?

- -

Plan
How can I use the information I am given?
Which strategy should I try?

- -

Solve
Did I follow the plan?
Did I show my work?
Did I write the answer?

- -

Check
Did I use the correct information?
Did I do what was asked?
Is my answer reasonable?

Facts Add.

6 + 6	3 + 8	5 + 9	2 + 3	4 + 9	3 + 4	8 + 9	2 + 7	0 + 3	4 + 4
4 + 8	2 + 9	7 + 8	4 + 5	9 + 1	2 + 6	5 + 5	6 + 7	3 + 7	9 + 9
7 + 9	2 + 4	6 + 5	3 + 3	6 + 9	4 + 7	0 + 0	2 + 2	3 + 9	5 + 8
3 + 6	8 + 8	4 + 6	2 + 5	6 + 8	3 + 5	5 + 7	10 + 10	2 + 8	7 + 7

Mental Math

a.	b.	c.	d.
e.	f.	g.	h.

Problem Solving

Understand

What information am I given?

What am I asked to find or do?

- -

Plan

How can I use the information I am given?

Which strategy should I try?

- -

Solve

Did I follow the plan?

Did I show my work?

Did I write the answer?

- -

Check

Did I use the correct information?

Did I do what was asked?

Is my answer reasonable?

Name _____ Time _____

Facts   Add.

6 +6	3 +8	5 +9	2 +3	4 +9	3 +4	8 +9	2 +7	0 +3	4 +4
4 +8	2 +9	7 +8	4 +5	9 +1	2 +6	5 +5	6 +7	3 +7	9 +9
7 +9	2 +4	6 +5	3 +3	6 +9	4 +7	0 +0	2 +2	3 +9	5 +8
3 +6	8 +8	4 +6	2 +5	6 +8	3 +5	5 +7	10 +10	2 +8	7 +7

Mental Math

a.	b.	c.	d.
e.	f.	g.	h.

Problem Solving

Understand

What information am I given?

What am I asked to find or do?

- -

Plan

How can I use the information I am given?

Which strategy should I try?

- -

Solve

Did I follow the plan?

Did I show my work?

Did I write the answer?

- -

Check

Did I use the correct information?

Did I do what was asked?

Is my answer reasonable?

Facts   Add.

6 + 6	3 + 8	5 + 9	2 + 3	4 + 9	3 + 4	8 + 9	2 + 7	0 + 3	4 + 4
4 + 8	2 + 9	7 + 8	4 + 5	9 + 1	2 + 6	5 + 5	6 + 7	3 + 7	9 + 9
7 + 9	2 + 4	6 + 5	3 + 3	6 + 9	4 + 7	0 + 0	2 + 2	3 + 9	5 + 8
3 + 6	8 + 8	4 + 6	2 + 5	6 + 8	3 + 5	5 + 7	10 + 10	2 + 8	7 + 7

Mental Math

a.	b.	c.	d.
e.	f.	g.	h.

Problem Solving

Understand

What information am I given?

What am I asked to find or do?

Plan

How can I use the information I am given?

Which strategy should I try?

Solve

Did I follow the plan?

Did I show my work?

Did I write the answer?

Check

Did I use the correct information?

Did I do what was asked?

Is my answer reasonable?

Facts   Add.

6 + 6	3 + 8	5 + 9	2 + 3	4 + 9	3 + 4	8 + 9	2 + 7	0 + 3	4 + 4
4 + 8	2 + 9	7 + 8	4 + 5	9 + 1	2 + 6	5 + 5	6 + 7	3 + 7	9 + 9
7 + 9	2 + 4	6 + 5	3 + 3	6 + 9	4 + 7	0 + 0	2 + 2	3 + 9	5 + 8
3 + 6	8 + 8	4 + 6	2 + 5	6 + 8	3 + 5	5 + 7	10 + 10	2 + 8	7 + 7

Mental Math

a.	**b.**	**c.**	**d.**
e.	**f.**	**g.**	**h.**

Problem Solving

Understand

What information am I given?
What am I asked to find or do?

Plan

How can I use the information I am given?
Which strategy should I try?

Solve

Did I follow the plan?
Did I show my work?
Did I write the answer?

Check

Did I use the correct information?
Did I do what was asked?
Is my answer reasonable?

Facts	Subtract.

11 − 9	6 − 0	13 − 6	10 − 3	15 − 7	9 − 6	12 − 9	8 − 2	14 − 7	5 − 3
5 − 2	10 − 8	14 − 6	9 − 4	7 − 5	17 − 8	6 − 3	10 − 5	12 − 6	8 − 3
13 − 4	11 − 6	16 − 8	12 − 7	9 − 5	13 − 5	8 − 4	14 − 5	8 − 8	9 − 7
15 − 6	6 − 2	10 − 4	17 − 9	16 − 7	7 − 4	12 − 8	4 − 2	18 − 9	11 − 8

Mental Math			

a.	b.	c.	d.
e.	f.	g.	h.

Problem Solving

Understand

What information am I given?

What am I asked to find or do?

Plan

How can I use the information I am given?

Which strategy should I try?

Solve

Did I follow the plan?

Did I show my work?

Did I write the answer?

Check

Did I use the correct information?

Did I do what was asked?

Is my answer reasonable?

Facts   Subtract.

11 − 9	6 − 0	13 − 6	10 − 3	15 − 7	9 − 6	12 − 9	8 − 2	14 − 7	5 − 3
5 − 2	10 − 8	14 − 6	9 − 4	7 − 5	17 − 8	6 − 3	10 − 5	12 − 6	8 − 3
13 − 4	11 − 6	16 − 8	12 − 7	9 − 5	13 − 5	8 − 4	14 − 5	8 − 8	9 − 7
15 − 6	6 − 2	10 − 4	17 − 9	16 − 7	7 − 4	12 − 8	4 − 2	18 − 9	11 − 8

Mental Math

a.	b.	c.	d.
e.	f.	g.	h.

Problem Solving

Understand

What information am I given?
What am I asked to find or do?

- -

Plan

How can I use the information I am given?
Which strategy should I try?

- -

Solve

Did I follow the plan?
Did I show my work?
Did I write the answer?

- -

Check

Did I use the correct information?
Did I do what was asked?
Is my answer reasonable?

Patterns of Multiples

1	2	3	4	5	6	7	8	9	10
11	12	13	14	15	16	17	18	19	20
21	22	23	24	25	26	27	28	29	30
31	32	33	34	35	36	37	38	39	40
41	42	43	44	45	46	47	48	49	50
51	52	53	54	55	56	57	58	59	60
61	62	63	64	65	66	67	68	69	70
71	72	73	74	75	76	77	78	79	80
81	82	83	84	85	86	87	88	89	90
91	92	93	94	95	96	97	98	99	100

Mental Math

a.	b.	c.	d.
e.	f.	g.	h.

Problem Solving

Understand

What information am I given?
What am I asked to find or do?

Plan

How can I use the information I am given?
Which strategy should I try?

Solve

Did I follow the plan?
Did I show my work?
Did I write the answer?

Check

Did I use the correct information?
Did I do what was asked?
Is my answer reasonable?

Facts   Add.

6 + 6	3 + 8	5 + 9	2 + 3	4 + 9	3 + 4	8 + 9	2 + 7	0 + 3	4 + 4
4 + 8	2 + 9	7 + 8	4 + 5	9 + 1	2 + 6	5 + 5	6 + 7	3 + 7	9 + 9
7 + 9	2 + 4	6 + 5	3 + 3	6 + 9	4 + 7	0 + 0	2 + 2	3 + 9	5 + 8
3 + 6	8 + 8	4 + 6	2 + 5	6 + 8	3 + 5	5 + 7	10 + 10	2 + 8	7 + 7

Mental Math

a.	b.	c.	d.
e.	f.	g.	h.

Problem Solving

Understand

What information am I given?

What am I asked to find or do?

- -

Plan

How can I use the information I am given?

Which strategy should I try?

- -

Solve

Did I follow the plan?

Did I show my work?

Did I write the answer?

- -

Check

Did I use the correct information?

Did I do what was asked?

Is my answer reasonable?

Facts — Add.

6 + 6	3 + 8	5 + 9	2 + 3	4 + 9	3 + 4	8 + 9	2 + 7	0 + 3	4 + 4
4 + 8	2 + 9	7 + 8	4 + 5	9 + 1	2 + 6	5 + 5	6 + 7	3 + 7	9 + 9
7 + 9	2 + 4	6 + 5	3 + 3	6 + 9	4 + 7	0 + 0	2 + 2	3 + 9	5 + 8
3 + 6	8 + 8	4 + 6	2 + 5	6 + 8	3 + 5	5 + 7	10 + 10	2 + 8	7 + 7

Mental Math

a.	**b.**	**c.**	**d.**
e.	**f.**	**g.**	**h.**

Problem Solving

Understand

What information am I given?

What am I asked to find or do?

- -

Plan

How can I use the information I am given?

Which strategy should I try?

- -

Solve

Did I follow the plan?

Did I show my work?

Did I write the answer?

- -

Check

Did I use the correct information?

Did I do what was asked?

Is my answer reasonable?

Patterns of Multiples

1	2	3	4	5	6	7	8	9	10
11	12	13	14	15	16	17	18	19	20
21	22	23	24	25	26	27	28	29	30
31	32	33	34	35	36	37	38	39	40
41	42	43	44	45	46	47	48	49	50
51	52	53	54	55	56	57	58	59	60
61	62	63	64	65	66	67	68	69	70
71	72	73	74	75	76	77	78	79	80
81	82	83	84	85	86	87	88	89	90
91	92	93	94	95	96	97	98	99	100

Mental Math

a.	b.	c.	d.
e.	f.	g.	h.

Problem Solving

Understand

What information am I given?

What am I asked to find or do?

- -

Plan

How can I use the information I am given?

Which strategy should I try?

- -

Solve

Did I follow the plan?

Did I show my work?

Did I write the answer?

- -

Check

Did I use the correct information?

Did I do what was asked?

Is my answer reasonable?

Patterns of Multiples

1	2	3	4	5	6	7	8	9	10
11	12	13	14	15	16	17	18	19	20
21	22	23	24	25	26	27	28	29	30
31	32	33	34	35	36	37	38	39	40
41	42	43	44	45	46	47	48	49	50
51	52	53	54	55	56	57	58	59	60
61	62	63	64	65	66	67	68	69	70
71	72	73	74	75	76	77	78	79	80
81	82	83	84	85	86	87	88	89	90
91	92	93	94	95	96	97	98	99	100

Mental Math

a.	b.	c.	d.
e.	f.	g.	h.

Problem Solving

Understand
What information am I given?
What am I asked to find or do?

- -

Plan
How can I use the information I am given?
Which strategy should I try?

- -

Solve
Did I follow the plan?
Did I show my work?
Did I write the answer?

- -

Check
Did I use the correct information?
Did I do what was asked?
Is my answer reasonable?

Facts Add.

6 + 6	3 + 8	5 + 9	2 + 3	4 + 9	3 + 4	8 + 9	2 + 7	0 + 3	4 + 4
4 + 8	2 + 9	7 + 8	4 + 5	9 + 1	2 + 6	5 + 5	6 + 7	3 + 7	9 + 9
7 + 9	2 + 4	6 + 5	3 + 3	6 + 9	4 + 7	0 + 0	2 + 2	3 + 9	5 + 8
3 + 6	8 + 8	4 + 6	2 + 5	6 + 8	3 + 5	5 + 7	10 + 10	2 + 8	7 + 7

Mental Math

a.	b.	c.	d.
e.	**f.**	**g.**	**h.**

Problem Solving

Understand

What information am I given?
What am I asked to find or do?

- -

Plan

How can I use the information I am given?
Which strategy should I try?

- -

Solve

Did I follow the plan?
Did I show my work?
Did I write the answer?

- -

Check

Did I use the correct information?
Did I do what was asked?
Is my answer reasonable?

Patterns of Multiples

1	2	3	4	5	6	7	8	9	10
11	12	13	14	15	16	17	18	19	20
21	22	23	24	25	26	27	28	29	30
31	32	33	34	35	36	37	38	39	40
41	42	43	44	45	46	47	48	49	50
51	52	53	54	55	56	57	58	59	60
61	62	63	64	65	66	67	68	69	70
71	72	73	74	75	76	77	78	79	80
81	82	83	84	85	86	87	88	89	90
91	92	93	94	95	96	97	98	99	100

Mental Math

a.	b.	c.	d.
e.	f.	g.	h.

Problem Solving

Understand

What information am I given?
What am I asked to find or do?

- -

Plan

How can I use the information I am given?
Which strategy should I try?

- -

Solve

Did I follow the plan?
Did I show my work?
Did I write the answer?

- -

Check

Did I use the correct information?
Did I do what was asked?
Is my answer reasonable?

Facts   Subtract.

11 − 9	6 − 0	13 − 6	10 − 3	15 − 7	9 − 6	12 − 9	8 − 2	14 − 7	5 − 3
5 − 2	10 − 8	14 − 6	9 − 4	7 − 5	17 − 8	6 − 3	10 − 5	12 − 6	8 − 3
13 − 4	11 − 6	16 − 8	12 − 7	9 − 5	13 − 5	8 − 4	14 − 5	8 − 8	9 − 7
15 − 6	6 − 2	10 − 4	17 − 9	16 − 7	7 − 4	12 − 8	4 − 2	18 − 9	11 − 8

Mental Math

a.	b.	c.	d.
e.	f.	g.	h.

Problem Solving

Understand
What information am I given?
What am I asked to find or do?

Plan
How can I use the information I am given?
Which strategy should I try?

Solve
Did I follow the plan?
Did I show my work?
Did I write the answer?

Check
Did I use the correct information?
Did I do what was asked?
Is my answer reasonable?

Patterns of Multiples

1	2	3	4	5	6	7	8	9	10
11	12	13	14	15	16	17	18	19	20
21	22	23	24	25	26	27	28	29	30
31	32	33	34	35	36	37	38	39	40
41	42	43	44	45	46	47	48	49	50
51	52	53	54	55	56	57	58	59	60
61	62	63	64	65	66	67	68	69	70
71	72	73	74	75	76	77	78	79	80
81	82	83	84	85	86	87	88	89	90
91	92	93	94	95	96	97	98	99	100

Mental Math

a.	b.	c.	d.
e.	f.	g.	h.

Problem Solving

Understand

What information am I given?

What am I asked to find or do?

- -

Plan

How can I use the information I am given?

Which strategy should I try?

- -

Solve

Did I follow the plan?

Did I show my work?

Did I write the answer?

- -

Check

Did I use the correct information?

Did I do what was asked?

Is my answer reasonable?

Patterns of Multiples

1	2	3	4	5	6	7	8	9	10
11	12	13	14	15	16	17	18	19	20
21	22	23	24	25	26	27	28	29	30
31	32	33	34	35	36	37	38	39	40
41	42	43	44	45	46	47	48	49	50
51	52	53	54	55	56	57	58	59	60
61	62	63	64	65	66	67	68	69	70
71	72	73	74	75	76	77	78	79	80
81	82	83	84	85	86	87	88	89	90
91	92	93	94	95	96	97	98	99	100

Mental Math

a.	b.	c.	d.
e.	f.	g.	h.

Problem Solving

Understand

What information am I given?

What am I asked to find or do?

- -

Plan

How can I use the information I am given?

Which strategy should I try?

- -

Solve

Did I follow the plan?

Did I show my work?

Did I write the answer?

- -

Check

Did I use the correct information?

Did I do what was asked?

Is my answer reasonable?

Facts   Subtract.

11 − 9	6 − 0	13 − 6	10 − 3	15 − 7	9 − 6	12 − 9	8 − 2	14 − 7	5 − 3
5 − 2	10 − 8	14 − 6	9 − 4	7 − 5	17 − 8	6 − 3	10 − 5	12 − 6	8 − 3
13 − 4	11 − 6	16 − 8	12 − 7	9 − 5	13 − 5	8 − 4	14 − 5	8 − 8	9 − 7
15 − 6	6 − 2	10 − 4	17 − 9	16 − 7	7 − 4	12 − 8	4 − 2	18 − 9	11 − 8

Mental Math

a.	b.	c.	d.
e.	f.	g.	h.

Problem Solving

Understand
What information am I given?
What am I asked to find or do?

- -

Plan
How can I use the information I am given?
Which strategy should I try?

- -

Solve
Did I follow the plan?
Did I show my work?
Did I write the answer?

- -

Check
Did I use the correct information?
Did I do what was asked?
Is my answer reasonable?

Patterns of Multiples

1	2	3	4	5	6	7	8	9	10
11	12	13	14	15	16	17	18	19	20
21	22	23	24	25	26	27	28	29	30
31	32	33	34	35	36	37	38	39	40
41	42	43	44	45	46	47	48	49	50
51	52	53	54	55	56	57	58	59	60
61	62	63	64	65	66	67	68	69	70
71	72	73	74	75	76	77	78	79	80
81	82	83	84	85	86	87	88	89	90
91	92	93	94	95	96	97	98	99	100

Mental Math

a.	b.	c.	d.
e.	f.	g.	h.

Problem Solving

Understand
What information am I given?
What am I asked to find or do?

- -

Plan
How can I use the information I am given?
Which strategy should I try?

- -

Solve
Did I follow the plan?
Did I show my work?
Did I write the answer?

- -

Check
Did I use the correct information?
Did I do what was asked?
Is my answer reasonable?

Facts   Add.

6 + 6	3 + 8	5 + 9	2 + 3	4 + 9	3 + 4	8 + 9	2 + 7	0 + 3	4 + 4
4 + 8	2 + 9	7 + 8	4 + 5	9 + 1	2 + 6	5 + 5	6 + 7	3 + 7	9 + 9
7 + 9	2 + 4	6 + 5	3 + 3	6 + 9	4 + 7	0 + 0	2 + 2	3 + 9	5 + 8
3 + 6	8 + 8	4 + 6	2 + 5	6 + 8	3 + 5	5 + 7	10 + 10	2 + 8	7 + 7

Mental Math

a.	b.	c.	d.
e.	f.	g.	h.

Problem Solving

Understand
What information am I given?
What am I asked to find or do?

Plan
How can I use the information I am given?
Which strategy should I try?

Solve
Did I follow the plan?
Did I show my work?
Did I write the answer?

Check
Did I use the correct information?
Did I do what was asked?
Is my answer reasonable?

Patterns of Multiples

1	2	3	4	5	6	7	8	9	10
11	12	13	14	15	16	17	18	19	20
21	22	23	24	25	26	27	28	29	30
31	32	33	34	35	36	37	38	39	40
41	42	43	44	45	46	47	48	49	50
51	52	53	54	55	56	57	58	59	60
61	62	63	64	65	66	67	68	69	70
71	72	73	74	75	76	77	78	79	80
81	82	83	84	85	86	87	88	89	90
91	92	93	94	95	96	97	98	99	100

Mental Math

a.	b.	c.	d.
e.	f.	g.	h.

Problem Solving

Understand
What information am I given?
What am I asked to find or do?

Plan
How can I use the information I am given?
Which strategy should I try?

Solve
Did I follow the plan?
Did I show my work?
Did I write the answer?

Check
Did I use the correct information?
Did I do what was asked?
Is my answer reasonable?

Facts Subtract.

11 − 9	6 − 0	13 − 6	10 − 3	15 − 7	9 − 6	12 − 9	8 − 2	14 − 7	5 − 3
5 − 2	10 − 8	14 − 6	9 − 4	7 − 5	17 − 8	6 − 3	10 − 5	12 − 6	8 − 3
13 − 4	11 − 6	16 − 8	12 − 7	9 − 5	13 − 5	8 − 4	14 − 5	8 − 8	9 − 7
15 − 6	6 − 2	10 − 4	17 − 9	16 − 7	7 − 4	12 − 8	4 − 2	18 − 9	11 − 8

Mental Math

a.	b.	c.	d.
e.	**f.**	**g.**	**h.**

Problem Solving

Understand

What information am I given?
What am I asked to find or do?

- -

Plan

How can I use the information I am given?
Which strategy should I try?

- -

Solve

Did I follow the plan?
Did I show my work?
Did I write the answer?

- -

Check

Did I use the correct information?
Did I do what was asked?
Is my answer reasonable?

© Houghton Mifflin Harcourt Publishing Company and Stephen Hake

Facts   Subtract.

11 − 9	6 − 0	13 − 6	10 − 3	15 − 7	9 − 6	12 − 9	8 − 2	14 − 7	5 − 3
5 − 2	10 − 8	14 − 6	9 − 4	7 − 5	17 − 8	6 − 3	10 − 5	12 − 6	8 − 3
13 − 4	11 − 6	16 − 8	12 − 7	9 − 5	13 − 5	8 − 4	14 − 5	8 − 8	9 − 7
15 − 6	6 − 2	10 − 4	17 − 9	16 − 7	7 − 4	12 − 8	4 − 2	18 − 9	11 − 8

Mental Math

a.	b.	c.	d.
e.	f.	g.	h.

Problem Solving

Understand
What information am I given?
What am I asked to find or do?

Plan
How can I use the information I am given?
Which strategy should I try?

Solve
Did I follow the plan?
Did I show my work?
Did I write the answer?

Check
Did I use the correct information?
Did I do what was asked?
Is my answer reasonable?

Facts   Subtract.

11 − 9	6 − 0	13 − 6	10 − 3	15 − 7	9 − 6	12 − 9	8 − 2	14 − 7	5 − 3
5 − 2	10 − 8	14 − 6	9 − 4	7 − 5	17 − 8	6 − 3	10 − 5	12 − 6	8 − 3
13 − 4	11 − 6	16 − 8	12 − 7	9 − 5	13 − 5	8 − 4	14 − 5	8 − 8	9 − 7
15 − 6	6 − 2	10 − 4	17 − 9	16 − 7	7 − 4	12 − 8	4 − 2	18 − 9	11 − 8

Mental Math

a.	**b.**	**c.**	**d.**
e.	**f.**	**g.**	**h.**

Problem Solving

Understand

What information am I given?

What am I asked to find or do?

Plan

How can I use the information I am given?

Which strategy should I try?

Solve

Did I follow the plan?

Did I show my work?

Did I write the answer?

Check

Did I use the correct information?

Did I do what was asked?

Is my answer reasonable?

Facts   Subtract.

11 − 9	6 − 0	13 − 6	10 − 3	15 − 7	9 − 6	12 − 9	8 − 2	14 − 7	5 − 3
5 − 2	10 − 8	14 − 6	9 − 4	7 − 5	17 − 8	6 − 3	10 − 5	12 − 6	8 − 3
13 − 4	11 − 6	16 − 8	12 − 7	9 − 5	13 − 5	8 − 4	14 − 5	8 − 8	9 − 7
15 − 6	6 − 2	10 − 4	17 − 9	16 − 7	7 − 4	12 − 8	4 − 2	18 − 9	11 − 8

Mental Math

a.	b.	c.	d.
e.	f.	g.	h.

Problem Solving

Understand

What information am I given?

What am I asked to find or do?

Plan

How can I use the information I am given?

Which strategy should I try?

Solve

Did I follow the plan?

Did I show my work?

Did I write the answer?

Check

Did I use the correct information?

Did I do what was asked?

Is my answer reasonable?

Facts   Add.

6 + 6	3 + 8	5 + 9	2 + 3	4 + 9	3 + 4	8 + 9	2 + 7	0 + 3	4 + 4
4 + 8	2 + 9	7 + 8	4 + 5	9 + 1	2 + 6	5 + 5	6 + 7	3 + 7	9 + 9
7 + 9	2 + 4	6 + 5	3 + 3	6 + 9	4 + 7	0 + 0	2 + 2	3 + 9	5 + 8
3 + 6	8 + 8	4 + 6	2 + 5	6 + 8	3 + 5	5 + 7	10 + 10	2 + 8	7 + 7

Mental Math

a.	**b.**	**c.**	**d.**
e.	**f.**	**g.**	**h.**

Problem Solving

Understand

What information am I given?

What am I asked to find or do?

- -

Plan

How can I use the information I am given?

Which strategy should I try?

- -

Solve

Did I follow the plan?

Did I show my work?

Did I write the answer?

- -

Check

Did I use the correct information?

Did I do what was asked?

Is my answer reasonable?

Facts   Subtract.

11 − 9	6 − 0	13 − 6	10 − 3	15 − 7	9 − 6	12 − 9	8 − 2	14 − 7	5 − 3
5 − 2	10 − 8	14 − 6	9 − 4	7 − 5	17 − 8	6 − 3	10 − 5	12 − 6	8 − 3
13 − 4	11 − 6	16 − 8	12 − 7	9 − 5	13 − 5	8 − 4	14 − 5	8 − 8	9 − 7
15 − 6	6 − 2	10 − 4	17 − 9	16 − 7	7 − 4	12 − 8	4 − 2	18 − 9	11 − 8

Mental Math

a.	b.	c.	d.
e.	f.	g.	h.

Problem Solving

Understand

What information am I given?

What am I asked to find or do?

- -

Plan

How can I use the information I am given?

Which strategy should I try?

- -

Solve

Did I follow the plan?

Did I show my work?

Did I write the answer?

- -

Check

Did I use the correct information?

Did I do what was asked?

Is my answer reasonable?

Facts Subtract.

11 − 9	6 − 0	13 − 6	10 − 3	15 − 7	9 − 6	12 − 9	8 − 2	14 − 7	5 − 3
5 − 2	10 − 8	14 − 6	9 − 4	7 − 5	17 − 8	6 − 3	10 − 5	12 − 6	8 − 3
13 − 4	11 − 6	16 − 8	12 − 7	9 − 5	13 − 5	8 − 4	14 − 5	8 − 8	9 − 7
15 − 6	6 − 2	10 − 4	17 − 9	16 − 7	7 − 4	12 − 8	4 − 2	18 − 9	11 − 8

Mental Math

a.	b.	c.	d.
e.	f.	g.	h.

Problem Solving

Understand
What information am I given?
What am I asked to find or do?

Plan
How can I use the information I am given?
Which strategy should I try?

Solve
Did I follow the plan?
Did I show my work?
Did I write the answer?

Check
Did I use the correct information?
Did I do what was asked?
Is my answer reasonable?

Facts   Subtract.

11 − 9	6 − 0	13 − 6	10 − 3	15 − 7	9 − 6	12 − 9	8 − 2	14 − 7	5 − 3
5 − 2	10 − 8	14 − 6	9 − 4	7 − 5	17 − 8	6 − 3	10 − 5	12 − 6	8 − 3
13 − 4	11 − 6	16 − 8	12 − 7	9 − 5	13 − 5	8 − 4	14 − 5	8 − 8	9 − 7
15 − 6	6 − 2	10 − 4	17 − 9	16 − 7	7 − 4	12 − 8	4 − 2	18 − 9	11 − 8

Mental Math

a.	**b.**	**c.**	**d.**
e.	**f.**	**g.**	**h.**

Problem Solving

Understand

What information am I given?

What am I asked to find or do?

- -

Plan

How can I use the information I am given?

Which strategy should I try?

- -

Solve

Did I follow the plan?

Did I show my work?

Did I write the answer?

- -

Check

Did I use the correct information?

Did I do what was asked?

Is my answer reasonable?

Name _____ Time _____

Facts Subtract.

11 − 9	6 − 0	13 − 6	10 − 3	15 − 7	9 − 6	12 − 9	8 − 2	14 − 7	5 − 3
5 − 2	10 − 8	14 − 6	9 − 4	7 − 5	17 − 8	6 − 3	10 − 5	12 − 6	8 − 3
13 − 4	11 − 6	16 − 8	12 − 7	9 − 5	13 − 5	8 − 4	14 − 5	8 − 8	9 − 7
15 − 6	6 − 2	10 − 4	17 − 9	16 − 7	7 − 4	12 − 8	4 − 2	18 − 9	11 − 8

Mental Math

a.	b.	c.	d.
e.	f.	g.	h.

Problem Solving

Understand
What information am I given?
What am I asked to find or do?

- -

Plan
How can I use the information I am given?
Which strategy should I try?

- -

Solve
Did I follow the plan?
Did I show my work?
Did I write the answer?

- -

Check
Did I use the correct information?
Did I do what was asked?
Is my answer reasonable?

Facts   Multiply.

5 ×5	1 ×8	0 ×6	9 ×2	5 ×4	1 ×1	2 ×3	5 ×3	3 ×0	1 ×9
9 ×0	8 ×5	1 ×5	6 ×5	1 ×0	4 ×2	4 ×5	7 ×0	2 ×7	6 ×1
6 ×2	5 ×0	2 ×2	1 ×3	5 ×6	5 ×7	0 ×0	8 ×2	9 ×5	4 ×1
2 ×1	5 ×8	0 ×2	3 ×5	5 ×9	8 ×0	1 ×7	2 ×5	0 ×4	7 ×5

Mental Math

a.	b.	c.	d.
e.	f.	g.	h.

Problem Solving

Understand
What information am I given?
What am I asked to find or do?

Plan
How can I use the information I am given?
Which strategy should I try?

Solve
Did I follow the plan?
Did I show my work?
Did I write the answer?

Check
Did I use the correct information?
Did I do what was asked?
Is my answer reasonable?

Facts   Add.

6 + 6	3 + 8	5 + 9	2 + 3	4 + 9	3 + 4	8 + 9	2 + 7	0 + 3	4 + 4
4 + 8	2 + 9	7 + 8	4 + 5	9 + 1	2 + 6	5 + 5	6 + 7	3 + 7	9 + 9
7 + 9	2 + 4	6 + 5	3 + 3	6 + 9	4 + 7	0 + 0	2 + 2	3 + 9	5 + 8
3 + 6	8 + 8	4 + 6	2 + 5	6 + 8	3 + 5	5 + 7	10 + 10	2 + 8	7 + 7

Mental Math

a.	b.	c.	d.
e.	**f.**	**g.**	**h.**

Problem Solving

Understand

What information am I given?
What am I asked to find or do?

- -

Plan

How can I use the information I am given?
Which strategy should I try?

- -

Solve

Did I follow the plan?
Did I show my work?
Did I write the answer?

- -

Check

Did I use the correct information?
Did I do what was asked?
Is my answer reasonable?

Facts   Multiply.

5 ×5	1 ×8	0 ×6	9 ×2	5 ×4	1 ×1	2 ×3	5 ×3	3 ×0	1 ×9
9 ×0	8 ×5	1 ×5	6 ×5	1 ×0	4 ×2	4 ×5	7 ×0	2 ×7	6 ×1
6 ×2	5 ×0	2 ×2	1 ×3	5 ×6	5 ×7	0 ×0	8 ×2	9 ×5	4 ×1
2 ×1	5 ×8	0 ×2	3 ×5	5 ×9	8 ×0	1 ×7	2 ×5	0 ×4	7 ×5

Mental Math

a.	**b.**	**c.**	**d.**
e.	**f.**	**g.**	**h.**

Problem Solving

Understand
What information am I given?
What am I asked to find or do?

Plan
How can I use the information I am given?
Which strategy should I try?

Solve
Did I follow the plan?
Did I show my work?
Did I write the answer?

Check
Did I use the correct information?
Did I do what was asked?
Is my answer reasonable?

Facts   Multiply.

5 × 5	1 × 8	0 × 6	9 × 2	5 × 4	1 × 1	2 × 3	5 × 3	3 × 0	1 × 9
9 × 0	8 × 5	1 × 5	6 × 5	1 × 0	4 × 2	4 × 5	7 × 0	2 × 7	6 × 1
6 × 2	5 × 0	2 × 2	1 × 3	5 × 6	5 × 7	0 × 0	8 × 2	9 × 5	4 × 1
2 × 1	5 × 8	0 × 2	3 × 5	5 × 9	8 × 0	1 × 7	2 × 5	0 × 4	7 × 5

Mental Math

a.	b.	c.	d.
e.	f.	g.	h.

Problem Solving

Understand
What information am I given?
What am I asked to find or do?

- -

Plan
How can I use the information I am given?
Which strategy should I try?

- -

Solve
Did I follow the plan?
Did I show my work?
Did I write the answer?

- -

Check
Did I use the correct information?
Did I do what was asked?
Is my answer reasonable?

Facts   Multiply.

8 × 8	2 × 9	1 × 2	5 × 7	1 × 5	5 × 3	1 × 1	5 × 6	5 × 2	6 × 6
9 × 5	3 × 3	6 × 5	2 × 4	6 × 2	7 × 9	5 × 8	3 × 2	2 × 7	4 × 5
8 × 2	2 × 5	2 × 6	2 × 2	10 × 10	7 × 5	0 × 2	5 × 5	5 × 4	5 × 9
7 × 7	0 × 0	7 × 2	8 × 5	4 × 2	0 × 5	2 × 8	9 × 2	3 × 5	4 × 4

Mental Math

a.	**b.**	**c.**	**d.**
e.	**f.**	**g.**	**h.**

Problem Solving

Understand

What information am I given?

What am I asked to find or do?

- -

Plan

How can I use the information I am given?

Which strategy should I try?

- -

Solve

Did I follow the plan?

Did I show my work?

Did I write the answer?

- -

Check

Did I use the correct information?

Did I do what was asked?

Is my answer reasonable?

Facts   Multiply.

8 × 8	2 × 9	1 × 2	5 × 7	1 × 5	5 × 3	1 × 1	5 × 6	5 × 2	6 × 6
9 × 5	3 × 3	6 × 5	2 × 4	6 × 2	7 × 9	5 × 8	3 × 2	2 × 7	4 × 5
8 × 2	2 × 5	2 × 6	2 × 2	10 × 10	7 × 5	0 × 2	5 × 5	5 × 4	5 × 9
7 × 7	0 × 0	7 × 2	8 × 5	4 × 2	0 × 5	2 × 8	9 × 2	3 × 5	4 × 4

Mental Math

a.	b.	c.	d.
e.	f.	g.	h.

Problem Solving

Understand

What information am I given?

What am I asked to find or do?

- -

Plan

How can I use the information I am given?

Which strategy should I try?

- -

Solve

Did I follow the plan?

Did I show my work?

Did I write the answer?

- -

Check

Did I use the correct information?

Did I do what was asked?

Is my answer reasonable?

Facts   Multiply.

6 × 6	7 × 5	9 × 4	1 × 2	0 × 5	6 × 9	3 × 3	9 × 2	5 × 6	7 × 7
4 × 2	7 × 9	5 × 5	2 × 9	8 × 5	5 × 2	8 × 9	6 × 5	8 × 2	9 × 7
3 × 5	2 × 2	4 × 9	7 × 2	9 × 8	9 × 5	5 × 7	3 × 2	9 × 3	1 × 9
8 × 8	0 × 9	1 × 5	5 × 8	2 × 6	3 × 9	4 × 5	9 × 6	4 × 4	9 × 9

Mental Math

a.	b.	c.	d.
e.	**f.**	**g.**	**h.**

Problem Solving

Understand
What information am I given?
What am I asked to find or do?

- -

Plan
How can I use the information I am given?
Which strategy should I try?

- -

Solve
Did I follow the plan?
Did I show my work?
Did I write the answer?

- -

Check
Did I use the correct information?
Did I do what was asked?
Is my answer reasonable?

Name _____ Time _____

Facts   Multiply.

8 ×8	2 ×9	1 ×2	5 ×7	1 ×5	5 ×3	1 ×1	5 ×6	5 ×2	6 ×6
9 ×5	3 ×3	6 ×5	2 ×4	6 ×2	7 ×9	5 ×8	3 ×2	2 ×7	4 ×5
8 ×2	2 ×5	2 ×6	2 ×2	10 ×10	7 ×5	0 ×2	5 ×5	5 ×4	5 ×9
7 ×7	0 ×0	7 ×2	8 ×5	4 ×2	0 ×5	2 ×8	9 ×2	3 ×5	4 ×4

Mental Math

a.	b.	c.	d.
e.	f.	g.	h.

Problem Solving

Understand
What information am I given?
What am I asked to find or do?

Plan
How can I use the information I am given?
Which strategy should I try?

Solve
Did I follow the plan?
Did I show my work?
Did I write the answer?

Check
Did I use the correct information?
Did I do what was asked?
Is my answer reasonable?

Facts   Multiply.

6 × 6	7 × 5	9 × 4	1 × 2	0 × 5	6 × 9	3 × 3	9 × 2	5 × 6	7 × 7
4 × 2	7 × 9	5 × 5	2 × 9	8 × 5	5 × 2	8 × 9	6 × 5	8 × 2	9 × 7
3 × 5	2 × 2	4 × 9	7 × 2	9 × 8	9 × 5	5 × 7	3 × 2	9 × 3	1 × 9
8 × 8	0 × 9	1 × 5	5 × 8	2 × 6	3 × 9	4 × 5	9 × 6	4 × 4	9 × 9

Mental Math

a.	b.	c.	d.
e.	**f.**	**g.**	**h.**

Problem Solving

Understand

What information am I given?

What am I asked to find or do?

- -

Plan

How can I use the information I am given?

Which strategy should I try?

- -

Solve

Did I follow the plan?

Did I show my work?

Did I write the answer?

- -

Check

Did I use the correct information?

Did I do what was asked?

Is my answer reasonable?

Facts   Multiply.

6 × 6	7 × 5	9 × 4	1 × 2	0 × 5	6 × 9	3 × 3	9 × 2	5 × 6	7 × 7
4 × 2	7 × 9	5 × 5	2 × 9	8 × 5	5 × 2	8 × 9	6 × 5	8 × 2	9 × 7
3 × 5	2 × 2	4 × 9	7 × 2	9 × 8	9 × 5	5 × 7	3 × 2	9 × 3	1 × 9
8 × 8	0 × 9	1 × 5	5 × 8	2 × 6	3 × 9	4 × 5	9 × 6	4 × 4	9 × 9

Mental Math

a.	b.	c.	d.
e.	f.	g.	h.

Problem Solving

Understand

What information am I given?
What am I asked to find or do?

Plan

How can I use the information I am given?
Which strategy should I try?

Solve

Did I follow the plan?
Did I show my work?
Did I write the answer?

Check

Did I use the correct information?
Did I do what was asked?
Is my answer reasonable?

Facts Multiply.

6 ×6	7 ×5	9 ×4	1 ×2	0 ×5	6 ×9	3 ×3	9 ×2	5 ×6	7 ×7
4 ×2	7 ×9	5 ×5	2 ×9	8 ×5	5 ×2	8 ×9	6 ×5	8 ×2	9 ×7
3 ×5	2 ×2	4 ×9	7 ×2	9 ×8	9 ×5	5 ×7	3 ×2	9 ×3	1 ×9
8 ×8	0 ×9	1 ×5	5 ×8	2 ×6	3 ×9	4 ×5	9 ×6	4 ×4	9 ×9

Mental Math

a.	**b.**	**c.**	**d.**
e.	**f.**	**g.**	**h.**

Problem Solving

Understand

What information am I given?

What am I asked to find or do?

- -

Plan

How can I use the information I am given?

Which strategy should I try?

- -

Solve

Did I follow the plan?

Did I show my work?

Did I write the answer?

- -

Check

Did I use the correct information?

Did I do what was asked?

Is my answer reasonable?

Facts   Multiply.

8 $\times 7$	6 $\times 3$	8 $\times 4$	8 $\times 3$	8 $\times 6$
4 $\times 3$	7 $\times 4$	7 $\times 3$	7 $\times 6$	6 $\times 4$
3 $\times 7$	4 $\times 6$	4 $\times 8$	6 $\times 8$	3 $\times 4$
6 $\times 7$	7 $\times 8$	3 $\times 6$	3 $\times 8$	4 $\times 7$

Mental Math

a.	b.	c.	d.
e.	f.	g.	h.

Problem Solving

Understand

What information am I given?

What am I asked to find or do?

- -

Plan

How can I use the information I am given?

Which strategy should I try?

- -

Solve

Did I follow the plan?

Did I show my work?

Did I write the answer?

- -

Check

Did I use the correct information?

Did I do what was asked?

Is my answer reasonable?

Facts   Multiply.

6 ×6	7 ×5	9 ×4	1 ×2	0 ×5	6 ×9	3 ×3	9 ×2	5 ×6	7 ×7
4 ×2	7 ×9	5 ×5	2 ×9	8 ×5	5 ×2	8 ×9	6 ×5	8 ×2	9 ×7
3 ×5	2 ×2	4 ×9	7 ×2	9 ×8	9 ×5	5 ×7	3 ×2	9 ×3	1 ×9
8 ×8	0 ×9	1 ×5	5 ×8	2 ×6	3 ×9	4 ×5	9 ×6	4 ×4	9 ×9

Mental Math

a.	b.	c.	d.
e.	f.	g.	h.

Problem Solving

Understand
What information am I given?
What am I asked to find or do?

Plan
How can I use the information I am given?
Which strategy should I try?

Solve
Did I follow the plan?
Did I show my work?
Did I write the answer?

Check
Did I use the correct information?
Did I do what was asked?
Is my answer reasonable?

Facts   Multiply.

8 × 7	6 × 3	8 × 4	8 × 3	8 × 6
4 × 3	7 × 4	7 × 3	7 × 6	6 × 4
3 × 7	4 × 6	4 × 8	6 × 8	3 × 4
6 × 7	7 × 8	3 × 6	3 × 8	4 × 7

Mental Math

a.	b.	c.	d.
e.	f.	g.	h.

Problem Solving

Understand

What information am I given?

What am I asked to find or do?

- -

Plan

How can I use the information I am given?

Which strategy should I try?

- -

Solve

Did I follow the plan?

Did I show my work?

Did I write the answer?

- -

Check

Did I use the correct information?

Did I do what was asked?

Is my answer reasonable?

Facts Multiply.

8 × 7	6 × 3	8 × 4	8 × 3	8 × 6
4 × 3	7 × 4	7 × 3	7 × 6	6 × 4
3 × 7	4 × 6	4 × 8	6 × 8	3 × 4
6 × 7	7 × 8	3 × 6	3 × 8	4 × 7

Mental Math

a.	b.	c.	d.
e.	f.	g.	h.

Problem Solving

Understand

What information am I given?

What am I asked to find or do?

- -

Plan

How can I use the information I am given?

Which strategy should I try?

- -

Solve

Did I follow the plan?

Did I show my work?

Did I write the answer?

- -

Check

Did I use the correct information?

Did I do what was asked?

Is my answer reasonable?

Facts   Multiply.

8 × 7	6 × 3	8 × 4	8 × 3	8 × 6
4 × 3	7 × 4	7 × 3	7 × 6	6 × 4
3 × 7	4 × 6	4 × 8	6 × 8	3 × 4
6 × 7	7 × 8	3 × 6	3 × 8	4 × 7

Mental Math

a.	b.	c.	d.
e.	f.	g.	h.

Problem Solving

Understand

What information am I given?

What am I asked to find or do?

- -

Plan

How can I use the information I am given?

Which strategy should I try?

- -

Solve

Did I follow the plan?

Did I show my work?

Did I write the answer?

- -

Check

Did I use the correct information?

Did I do what was asked?

Is my answer reasonable?

Facts   Multiply.

9 × 9	1 × 8	4 × 4	2 × 5	7 × 9	5 × 5	3 × 4	4 × 6	2 × 9	6 × 9
6 × 6	2 × 7	5 × 8	3 × 9	6 × 8	8 × 9	2 × 2	7 × 8	3 × 7	7 × 6
3 × 6	10 × 10	2 × 3	5 × 6	4 × 9	3 × 8	4 × 7	5 × 9	0 × 4	2 × 6
2 × 8	4 × 5	6 × 7	3 × 3	5 × 7	2 × 4	8 × 8	3 × 5	4 × 8	7 × 7

Mental Math

a.	**b.**	**c.**	**d.**
e.	**f.**	**g.**	**h.**

Problem Solving

Understand

What information am I given?

What am I asked to find or do?

- -

Plan

How can I use the information I am given?

Which strategy should I try?

- -

Solve

Did I follow the plan?

Did I show my work?

Did I write the answer?

- -

Check

Did I use the correct information?

Did I do what was asked?

Is my answer reasonable?

Facts   Multiply.

9 × 9	1 × 8	4 × 4	2 × 5	7 × 9	5 × 5	3 × 4	4 × 6	2 × 9	6 × 9
6 × 6	2 × 7	5 × 8	3 × 9	6 × 8	8 × 9	2 × 2	7 × 8	3 × 7	7 × 6
3 × 6	10 × 10	2 × 3	5 × 6	4 × 9	3 × 8	4 × 7	5 × 9	0 × 4	2 × 6
2 × 8	4 × 5	6 × 7	3 × 3	5 × 7	2 × 4	8 × 8	3 × 5	4 × 8	7 × 7

Mental Math

a.	b.	c.	d.
e.	f.	g.	h.

Problem Solving

Understand

What information am I given?

What am I asked to find or do?

- -

Plan

How can I use the information I am given?

Which strategy should I try?

- -

Solve

Did I follow the plan?

Did I show my work?

Did I write the answer?

- -

Check

Did I use the correct information?

Did I do what was asked?

Is my answer reasonable?

Facts Multiply.

8 ×8	0 ×5	7 ×3	9 ×7	3 ×2	9 ×4	8 ×6	4 ×3	9 ×5	6 ×2
9 ×2	7 ×4	8 ×3	5 ×5	9 ×6	7 ×2	5 ×4	9 ×1	9 ×3	0 ×0
7 ×5	2 ×2	6 ×4	8 ×7	5 ×3	7 ×6	4 ×2	8 ×5	6 ×3	9 ×9
3 ×3	8 ×4	7 ×7	8 ×2	10 ×10	6 ×5	4 ×4	9 ×8	5 ×2	6 ×6

Mental Math

a.	b.	c.	d.
e.	f.	g.	h.

Problem Solving

Understand

What information am I given?
What am I asked to find or do?

Plan

How can I use the information I am given?
Which strategy should I try?

Solve

Did I follow the plan?
Did I show my work?
Did I write the answer?

Check

Did I use the correct information?
Did I do what was asked?
Is my answer reasonable?

Facts   Multiply.

8 × 8	0 × 5	7 × 3	9 × 7	3 × 2	9 × 4	8 × 6	4 × 3	9 × 5	6 × 2
9 × 2	7 × 4	8 × 3	5 × 5	9 × 6	7 × 2	5 × 4	9 × 1	9 × 3	0 × 0
7 × 5	2 × 2	6 × 4	8 × 7	5 × 3	7 × 6	4 × 2	8 × 5	6 × 3	9 × 9
3 × 3	8 × 4	7 × 7	8 × 2	10 × 10	6 × 5	4 × 4	9 × 8	5 × 2	6 × 6

Mental Math

a.	b.	c.	d.
e.	f.	g.	h.

Problem Solving

Understand

What information am I given?

What am I asked to find or do?

- -

Plan

How can I use the information I am given?

Which strategy should I try?

- -

Solve

Did I follow the plan?

Did I show my work?

Did I write the answer?

- -

Check

Did I use the correct information?

Did I do what was asked?

Is my answer reasonable?

Facts   Divide.

9)81	3)27	5)25	2)6	5)45	3)9	4)32	4)16	2)12	7)56
1)9	6)42	2)14	4)28	3)24	5)40	2)18	8)72	3)18	6)54
7)49	2)8	6)36	3)12	8)64	2)4	5)0	4)24	8)8	5)35
3)21	4)20	2)16	5)30	4)36	3)15	6)48	2)10	7)63	8)56

Mental Math

a.	**b.**	**c.**	**d.**
e.	**f.**	**g.**	**h.**

Problem Solving

Understand

What information am I given?
What am I asked to find or do?

- -

Plan

How can I use the information I am given?
Which strategy should I try?

- -

Solve

Did I follow the plan?
Did I show my work?
Did I write the answer?

- -

Check

Did I use the correct information?
Did I do what was asked?
Is my answer reasonable?

Facts   Divide.

9)81	3)27	5)25	2)6	5)45	3)9	4)32	4)16	2)12	7)56
1)9	6)42	2)14	4)28	3)24	5)40	2)18	8)72	3)18	6)54
7)49	2)8	6)36	3)12	8)64	2)4	5)0	4)24	8)8	5)35
3)21	4)20	2)16	5)30	4)36	3)15	6)48	2)10	7)63	8)56

Mental Math

a.	b.	c.	d.
e.	f.	g.	h.

Problem Solving

Understand

What information am I given?

What am I asked to find or do?

- -

Plan

How can I use the information I am given?

Which strategy should I try?

- -

Solve

Did I follow the plan?

Did I show my work?

Did I write the answer?

- -

Check

Did I use the correct information?

Did I do what was asked?

Is my answer reasonable?

Facts · Divide.

$9\overline{)81}$	$3\overline{)27}$	$5\overline{)25}$	$2\overline{)6}$	$5\overline{)45}$	$3\overline{)9}$	$4\overline{)32}$	$4\overline{)16}$	$2\overline{)12}$	$7\overline{)56}$
$1\overline{)9}$	$6\overline{)42}$	$2\overline{)14}$	$4\overline{)28}$	$3\overline{)24}$	$5\overline{)40}$	$2\overline{)18}$	$8\overline{)72}$	$3\overline{)18}$	$6\overline{)54}$
$7\overline{)49}$	$2\overline{)8}$	$6\overline{)36}$	$3\overline{)12}$	$8\overline{)64}$	$2\overline{)4}$	$5\overline{)0}$	$4\overline{)24}$	$8\overline{)8}$	$5\overline{)35}$
$3\overline{)21}$	$4\overline{)20}$	$2\overline{)16}$	$5\overline{)30}$	$4\overline{)36}$	$3\overline{)15}$	$6\overline{)48}$	$2\overline{)10}$	$7\overline{)63}$	$8\overline{)56}$

Mental Math

a.	b.	c.	d.
e.	f.	g.	h.

Problem Solving

Understand

What information am I given?
What am I asked to find or do?

- -

Plan

How can I use the information I am given?
Which strategy should I try?

- -

Solve

Did I follow the plan?
Did I show my work?
Did I write the answer?

- -

Check

Did I use the correct information?
Did I do what was asked?
Is my answer reasonable?

Facts	Divide.

9)81	3)27	5)25	2)6	5)45	3)9	4)32	4)16	2)12	7)56
1)9	6)42	2)14	4)28	3)24	5)40	2)18	8)72	3)18	6)54
7)49	2)8	6)36	3)12	8)64	2)4	5)0	4)24	8)8	5)35
3)21	4)20	2)16	5)30	4)36	3)15	6)48	2)10	7)63	8)56

Mental Math

a.	b.	c.	d.
e.	f.	g.	h.

Problem Solving

Understand
What information am I given?
What am I asked to find or do?

Plan
How can I use the information I am given?
Which strategy should I try?

Solve
Did I follow the plan?
Did I show my work?
Did I write the answer?

Check
Did I use the correct information?
Did I do what was asked?
Is my answer reasonable?

Facts — Divide.

8)8	6)36	8)16	9)63	8)40	6)12	9)81	5)25	3)9	9)27
8)32	2)4	5)20	9)72	4)12	8)56	8)24	9)36	5)10	9)54
6)18	7)42	3)6	7)35	8)64	4)16	1)7	9)18	6)48	7)28
7)14	3)0	9)45	7)21	6)24	4)8	8)48	6)30	5)15	7)49

Mental Math

a.	b.	c.	d.
e.	f.	g.	h.

Problem Solving

Understand
What information am I given?
What am I asked to find or do?

Plan
How can I use the information I am given?
Which strategy should I try?

Solve
Did I follow the plan?
Did I show my work?
Did I write the answer?

Check
Did I use the correct information?
Did I do what was asked?
Is my answer reasonable?

Facts Divide.

8)8	6)36	8)16	9)63	8)40	6)12	9)81	5)25	3)9	9)27
8)32	2)4	5)20	9)72	4)12	8)56	8)24	9)36	5)10	9)54
6)18	7)42	3)6	7)35	8)64	4)16	1)7	9)18	6)48	7)28
7)14	3)0	9)45	7)21	6)24	4)8	8)48	6)30	5)15	7)49

Mental Math

a.	b.	c.	d.
e.	f.	g.	h.

Problem Solving

Understand

What information am I given?
What am I asked to find or do?

- -

Plan

How can I use the information I am given?
Which strategy should I try?

- -

Solve

Did I follow the plan?
Did I show my work?
Did I write the answer?

- -

Check

Did I use the correct information?
Did I do what was asked?
Is my answer reasonable?

Facts   Divide.

8)8	6)36	8)16	9)63	8)40	6)12	9)81	5)25	3)9	9)27
8)32	2)4	5)20	9)72	4)12	8)56	8)24	9)36	5)10	9)54
6)18	7)42	3)6	7)35	8)64	4)16	1)7	9)18	6)48	7)28
7)14	3)0	9)45	7)21	6)24	4)8	8)48	6)30	5)15	7)49

Mental Math

a.	b.	c.	d.
e.	f.	g.	h.

Problem Solving

Understand

What information am I given?
What am I asked to find or do?

- -

Plan

How can I use the information I am given?
Which strategy should I try?

- -

Solve

Did I follow the plan?
Did I show my work?
Did I write the answer?

- -

Check

Did I use the correct information?
Did I do what was asked?
Is my answer reasonable?

Facts   Divide.

$8\overline{)8}$	$6\overline{)36}$	$8\overline{)16}$	$9\overline{)63}$	$8\overline{)40}$	$6\overline{)12}$	$9\overline{)81}$	$5\overline{)25}$	$3\overline{)9}$	$9\overline{)27}$
$8\overline{)32}$	$2\overline{)4}$	$5\overline{)20}$	$9\overline{)72}$	$4\overline{)12}$	$8\overline{)56}$	$8\overline{)24}$	$9\overline{)36}$	$5\overline{)10}$	$9\overline{)54}$
$6\overline{)18}$	$7\overline{)42}$	$3\overline{)6}$	$7\overline{)35}$	$8\overline{)64}$	$4\overline{)16}$	$1\overline{)7}$	$9\overline{)18}$	$6\overline{)48}$	$7\overline{)28}$
$7\overline{)14}$	$3\overline{)0}$	$9\overline{)45}$	$7\overline{)21}$	$6\overline{)24}$	$4\overline{)8}$	$8\overline{)48}$	$6\overline{)30}$	$5\overline{)15}$	$7\overline{)49}$

Mental Math

a.	**b.**	**c.**	**d.**
e.	**f.**	**g.**	**h.**

Problem Solving

Understand

What information am I given?
What am I asked to find or do?

- -

Plan

How can I use the information I am given?
Which strategy should I try?

- -

Solve

Did I follow the plan?
Did I show my work?
Did I write the answer?

- -

Check

Did I use the correct information?
Did I do what was asked?
Is my answer reasonable?

Facts   Divide.

9)81	3)27	5)25	2)6	5)45	3)9	4)32	4)16	2)12	7)56
1)9	6)42	2)14	4)28	3)24	5)40	2)18	8)72	3)18	6)54
7)49	2)8	6)36	3)12	8)64	2)4	5)0	4)24	8)8	5)35
3)21	4)20	2)16	5)30	4)36	3)15	6)48	2)10	7)63	8)56

Mental Math

a.	b.	c.	d.
e.	f.	g.	h.

Problem Solving

Understand

What information am I given?
What am I asked to find or do?

- -

Plan

How can I use the information I am given?
Which strategy should I try?

- -

Solve

Did I follow the plan?
Did I show my work?
Did I write the answer?

- -

Check

Did I use the correct information?
Did I do what was asked?
Is my answer reasonable?

Facts   Divide.

$9\overline{)81}$	$3\overline{)27}$	$5\overline{)25}$	$2\overline{)6}$	$5\overline{)45}$	$3\overline{)9}$	$4\overline{)32}$	$4\overline{)16}$	$2\overline{)12}$	$7\overline{)56}$
$1\overline{)9}$	$6\overline{)42}$	$2\overline{)14}$	$4\overline{)28}$	$3\overline{)24}$	$5\overline{)40}$	$2\overline{)18}$	$8\overline{)72}$	$3\overline{)18}$	$6\overline{)54}$
$7\overline{)49}$	$2\overline{)8}$	$6\overline{)36}$	$3\overline{)12}$	$8\overline{)64}$	$2\overline{)4}$	$5\overline{)0}$	$4\overline{)24}$	$8\overline{)8}$	$5\overline{)35}$
$3\overline{)21}$	$4\overline{)20}$	$2\overline{)16}$	$5\overline{)30}$	$4\overline{)36}$	$3\overline{)15}$	$6\overline{)48}$	$2\overline{)10}$	$7\overline{)63}$	$8\overline{)56}$

Mental Math

a.	b.	c.	d.
e.	f.	g.	h.

Problem Solving

Understand

What information am I given?
What am I asked to find or do?

- -

Plan

How can I use the information I am given?
Which strategy should I try?

- -

Solve

Did I follow the plan?
Did I show my work?
Did I write the answer?

- -

Check

Did I use the correct information?
Did I do what was asked?
Is my answer reasonable?

Facts   Divide.

8)8	6)36	8)16	9)63	8)40	6)12	9)81	5)25	3)9	9)27
8)32	2)4	5)20	9)72	4)12	8)56	8)24	9)36	5)10	9)54
6)18	7)42	3)6	7)35	8)64	4)16	1)7	9)18	6)48	7)28
7)14	3)0	9)45	7)21	6)24	4)8	8)48	6)30	5)15	7)49

Mental Math

a.	**b.**	**c.**	**d.**
e.	**f.**	**g.**	**h.**

Problem Solving

Understand

What information am I given?

What am I asked to find or do?

- -

Plan

How can I use the information I am given?

Which strategy should I try?

- -

Solve

Did I follow the plan?

Did I show my work?

Did I write the answer?

- -

Check

Did I use the correct information?

Did I do what was asked?

Is my answer reasonable?

Facts — Divide.

8)8	6)36	8)16	9)63	8)40	6)12	9)81	5)25	3)9	9)27
8)32	2)4	5)20	9)72	4)12	8)56	8)24	9)36	5)10	9)54
6)18	7)42	3)6	7)35	8)64	4)16	1)7	9)18	6)48	7)28
7)14	3)0	9)45	7)21	6)24	4)8	8)48	6)30	5)15	7)49

Mental Math

a.	b.	c.	d.
e.	f.	g.	h.

Problem Solving

Understand

What information am I given?
What am I asked to find or do?

- -

Plan

How can I use the information I am given?
Which strategy should I try?

- -

Solve

Did I follow the plan?
Did I show my work?
Did I write the answer?

- -

Check

Did I use the correct information?
Did I do what was asked?
Is my answer reasonable?

Facts   Divide.

8)8	6)36	8)16	9)63	8)40	6)12	9)81	5)25	3)9	9)27
8)32	2)4	5)20	9)72	4)12	8)56	8)24	9)36	5)10	9)54
6)18	7)42	3)6	7)35	8)64	4)16	1)7	9)18	6)48	7)28
7)14	3)0	9)45	7)21	6)24	4)8	8)48	6)30	5)15	7)49

Mental Math

a.	b.	c.	d.
e.	f.	g.	h.

Problem Solving

Understand

What information am I given?
What am I asked to find or do?

- -

Plan

How can I use the information I am given?
Which strategy should I try?

- -

Solve

Did I follow the plan?
Did I show my work?
Did I write the answer?

- -

Check

Did I use the correct information?
Did I do what was asked?
Is my answer reasonable?

Facts Divide.

$8\overline{)8}$	$6\overline{)36}$	$8\overline{)16}$	$9\overline{)63}$	$8\overline{)40}$	$6\overline{)12}$	$9\overline{)81}$	$5\overline{)25}$	$3\overline{)9}$	$9\overline{)27}$
$8\overline{)32}$	$2\overline{)4}$	$5\overline{)20}$	$9\overline{)72}$	$4\overline{)12}$	$8\overline{)56}$	$8\overline{)24}$	$9\overline{)36}$	$5\overline{)10}$	$9\overline{)54}$
$6\overline{)18}$	$7\overline{)42}$	$3\overline{)6}$	$7\overline{)35}$	$8\overline{)64}$	$4\overline{)16}$	$1\overline{)7}$	$9\overline{)18}$	$6\overline{)48}$	$7\overline{)28}$
$7\overline{)14}$	$3\overline{)0}$	$9\overline{)45}$	$7\overline{)21}$	$6\overline{)24}$	$4\overline{)8}$	$8\overline{)48}$	$6\overline{)30}$	$5\overline{)15}$	$7\overline{)49}$

Mental Math

a.	**b.**	**c.**	**d.**
e.	**f.**	**g.**	**h.**

Problem Solving

Understand

What information am I given?

What am I asked to find or do?

- -

Plan

How can I use the information I am given?

Which strategy should I try?

- -

Solve

Did I follow the plan?

Did I show my work?

Did I write the answer?

- -

Check

Did I use the correct information?

Did I do what was asked?

Is my answer reasonable?

Facts   Divide.

9)81	3)27	5)25	2)6	5)45	3)9	4)32	4)16	2)12	7)56
1)9	6)42	2)14	4)28	3)24	5)40	2)18	8)72	3)18	6)54
7)49	2)8	6)36	3)12	8)64	2)4	5)0	4)24	8)8	5)35
3)21	4)20	2)16	5)30	4)36	3)15	6)48	2)10	7)63	8)56

Mental Math

a.	b.	c.	d.
e.	f.	g.	h.

Problem Solving

Understand

What information am I given?

What am I asked to find or do?

- -

Plan

How can I use the information I am given?

Which strategy should I try?

- -

Solve

Did I follow the plan?

Did I show my work?

Did I write the answer?

- -

Check

Did I use the correct information?

Did I do what was asked?

Is my answer reasonable?

For use with Lesson 68

| Facts | Divide. |

9)81	3)27	5)25	2)6	5)45	3)9	4)32	4)16	2)12	7)56
1)9	6)42	2)14	4)28	3)24	5)40	2)18	8)72	3)18	6)54
7)49	2)8	6)36	3)12	8)64	2)4	5)0	4)24	8)8	5)35
3)21	4)20	2)16	5)30	4)36	3)15	6)48	2)10	7)63	8)56

Mental Math

a.	b.	c.	d.
e.	f.	g.	h.

Problem Solving

Understand

What information am I given?
What am I asked to find or do?

- -

Plan

How can I use the information I am given?
Which strategy should I try?

- -

Solve

Did I follow the plan?
Did I show my work?
Did I write the answer?

- -

Check

Did I use the correct information?
Did I do what was asked?
Is my answer reasonable?

Facts   Divide.

9)81	3)27	5)25	2)6	5)45	3)9	4)32	4)16	2)12	7)56
1)9	6)42	2)14	4)28	3)24	5)40	2)18	8)72	3)18	6)54
7)49	2)8	6)36	3)12	8)64	2)4	5)0	4)24	8)8	5)35
3)21	4)20	2)16	5)30	4)36	3)15	6)48	2)10	7)63	8)56

Mental Math

a.	b.	c.	d.
e.	f.	g.	h.

Problem Solving

Understand

What information am I given?
What am I asked to find or do?

- -

Plan

How can I use the information I am given?
Which strategy should I try?

- -

Solve

Did I follow the plan?
Did I show my work?
Did I write the answer?

- -

Check

Did I use the correct information?
Did I do what was asked?
Is my answer reasonable?

Facts Divide.

9)81	3)27	5)25	2)6	5)45	3)9	4)32	4)16	2)12	7)56
1)9	6)42	2)14	4)28	3)24	5)40	2)18	8)72	3)18	6)54
7)49	2)8	6)36	3)12	8)64	2)4	5)0	4)24	8)8	5)35
3)21	4)20	2)16	5)30	4)36	3)15	6)48	2)10	7)63	8)56

Mental Math

a.	b.	c.	d.
e.	f.	g.	h.

Problem Solving

Understand
What information am I given?
What am I asked to find or do?

Plan
How can I use the information I am given?
Which strategy should I try?

Solve
Did I follow the plan?
Did I show my work?
Did I write the answer?

Check
Did I use the correct information?
Did I do what was asked?
Is my answer reasonable?

Facts Multiply.

8 ×8	0 ×5	7 ×3	9 ×7	3 ×2	9 ×4	8 ×6	4 ×3	9 ×5	6 ×2
9 ×2	7 ×4	8 ×3	5 ×5	9 ×6	7 ×2	5 ×4	9 ×1	9 ×3	0 ×0
7 ×5	2 ×2	6 ×4	8 ×7	5 ×3	7 ×6	4 ×2	8 ×5	6 ×3	9 ×9
3 ×3	8 ×4	7 ×7	8 ×2	10 ×10	6 ×5	4 ×4	9 ×8	5 ×2	6 ×6

Mental Math

a.	**b.**	**c.**	**d.**
e.	**f.**	**g.**	**h.**

Problem Solving

Understand

What information am I given?
What am I asked to find or do?

- -

Plan

How can I use the information I am given?
Which strategy should I try?

- -

Solve

Did I follow the plan?
Did I show my work?
Did I write the answer?

- -

Check

Did I use the correct information?
Did I do what was asked?
Is my answer reasonable?

Facts   Multiply.

8 × 8	0 × 5	7 × 3	9 × 7	3 × 2	9 × 4	8 × 6	4 × 3	9 × 5	6 × 2
9 × 2	7 × 4	8 × 3	5 × 5	9 × 6	7 × 2	5 × 4	9 × 1	9 × 3	0 × 0
7 × 5	2 × 2	6 × 4	8 × 7	5 × 3	7 × 6	4 × 2	8 × 5	6 × 3	9 × 9
3 × 3	8 × 4	7 × 7	8 × 2	10 × 10	6 × 5	4 × 4	9 × 8	5 × 2	6 × 6

Mental Math

a.	**b.**	**c.**	**d.**
e.	**f.**	**g.**	**h.**

Problem Solving

Understand

What information am I given?

What am I asked to find or do?

Plan

How can I use the information I am given?

Which strategy should I try?

Solve

Did I follow the plan?

Did I show my work?

Did I write the answer?

Check

Did I use the correct information?

Did I do what was asked?

Is my answer reasonable?

Facts   Multiply.

8 ×8	0 ×5	7 ×3	9 ×7	3 ×2	9 ×4	8 ×6	4 ×3	9 ×5	6 ×2
9 ×2	7 ×4	8 ×3	5 ×5	9 ×6	7 ×2	5 ×4	9 ×1	9 ×3	0 ×0
7 ×5	2 ×2	6 ×4	8 ×7	5 ×3	7 ×6	4 ×2	8 ×5	6 ×3	9 ×9
3 ×3	8 ×4	7 ×7	8 ×2	10 ×10	6 ×5	4 ×4	9 ×8	5 ×2	6 ×6

Mental Math

a.	b.	c.	d.
e.	f.	g.	h.

Problem Solving

Understand

What information am I given?

What am I asked to find or do?

- -

Plan

How can I use the information I am given?

Which strategy should I try?

- -

Solve

Did I follow the plan?

Did I show my work?

Did I write the answer?

- -

Check

Did I use the correct information?

Did I do what was asked?

Is my answer reasonable?

Facts   Multiply.

8 ×8	0 ×5	7 ×3	9 ×7	3 ×2	9 ×4	8 ×6	4 ×3	9 ×5	6 ×2
9 ×2	7 ×4	8 ×3	5 ×5	9 ×6	7 ×2	5 ×4	9 ×1	9 ×3	0 ×0
7 ×5	2 ×2	6 ×4	8 ×7	5 ×3	7 ×6	4 ×2	8 ×5	6 ×3	9 ×9
3 ×3	8 ×4	7 ×7	8 ×2	10 ×10	6 ×5	4 ×4	9 ×8	5 ×2	6 ×6

Mental Math

a.	b.	c.	d.
e.	f.	g.	h.

Problem Solving

Understand

What information am I given?
What am I asked to find or do?

- -

Plan

How can I use the information I am given?
Which strategy should I try?

- -

Solve

Did I follow the plan?
Did I show my work?
Did I write the answer?

- -

Check

Did I use the correct information?
Did I do what was asked?
Is my answer reasonable?

Facts   Multiply.

8 × 8	0 × 5	7 × 3	9 × 7	3 × 2	9 × 4	8 × 6	4 × 3	9 × 5	6 × 2
9 × 2	7 × 4	8 × 3	5 × 5	9 × 6	7 × 2	5 × 4	9 × 1	9 × 3	0 × 0
7 × 5	2 × 2	6 × 4	8 × 7	5 × 3	7 × 6	4 × 2	8 × 5	6 × 3	9 × 9
3 × 3	8 × 4	7 × 7	8 × 2	10 × 10	6 × 5	4 × 4	9 × 8	5 × 2	6 × 6

Mental Math

a.	b.	c.	d.
e.	f.	g.	h.

Problem Solving

Understand

What information am I given?

What am I asked to find or do?

- -

Plan

How can I use the information I am given?

Which strategy should I try?

- -

Solve

Did I follow the plan?

Did I show my work?

Did I write the answer?

- -

Check

Did I use the correct information?

Did I do what was asked?

Is my answer reasonable?

Facts   Multiply.

9 × 9	1 × 8	4 × 4	2 × 5	7 × 9	5 × 5	3 × 4	4 × 6	2 × 9	6 × 9
6 × 6	2 × 7	5 × 8	3 × 9	6 × 8	8 × 9	2 × 2	7 × 8	3 × 7	7 × 6
3 × 6	10 × 10	2 × 3	5 × 6	4 × 9	3 × 8	4 × 7	5 × 9	0 × 4	2 × 6
2 × 8	4 × 5	6 × 7	3 × 3	5 × 7	2 × 4	8 × 8	3 × 5	4 × 8	7 × 7

Mental Math

a.	b.	c.	d.
e.	f.	g.	h.

Problem Solving

Understand

What information am I given?

What am I asked to find or do?

- -

Plan

How can I use the information I am given?

Which strategy should I try?

- -

Solve

Did I follow the plan?

Did I show my work?

Did I write the answer?

- -

Check

Did I use the correct information?

Did I do what was asked?

Is my answer reasonable?

Facts   Multiply.

9 × 9	1 × 8	4 × 4	2 × 5	7 × 9	5 × 5	3 × 4	4 × 6	2 × 9	6 × 9
6 × 6	2 × 7	5 × 8	3 × 9	6 × 8	8 × 9	2 × 2	7 × 8	3 × 7	7 × 6
3 × 6	10 × 10	2 × 3	5 × 6	4 × 9	3 × 8	4 × 7	5 × 9	0 × 4	2 × 6
2 × 8	4 × 5	6 × 7	3 × 3	5 × 7	2 × 4	8 × 8	3 × 5	4 × 8	7 × 7

Mental Math

a.	b.	c.	d.
e.	f.	g.	h.

Problem Solving

Understand

What information am I given?
What am I asked to find or do?

Plan

How can I use the information I am given?
Which strategy should I try?

Solve

Did I follow the plan?
Did I show my work?
Did I write the answer?

Check

Did I use the correct information?
Did I do what was asked?
Is my answer reasonable?

Facts Multiply.

9 × 9	1 × 8	4 × 4	2 × 5	7 × 9	5 × 5	3 × 4	4 × 6	2 × 9	6 × 9
6 × 6	2 × 7	5 × 8	3 × 9	6 × 8	8 × 9	2 × 2	7 × 8	3 × 7	7 × 6
3 × 6	10 × 10	2 × 3	5 × 6	4 × 9	3 × 8	4 × 7	5 × 9	0 × 4	2 × 6
2 × 8	4 × 5	6 × 7	3 × 3	5 × 7	2 × 4	8 × 8	3 × 5	4 × 8	7 × 7

Mental Math

a.	b.	c.	d.
e.	f.	g.	h.

Problem Solving

Understand

What information am I given?

What am I asked to find or do?

- -

Plan

How can I use the information I am given?

Which strategy should I try?

- -

Solve

Did I follow the plan?

Did I show my work?

Did I write the answer?

- -

Check

Did I use the correct information?

Did I do what was asked?

Is my answer reasonable?

Facts　Multiply.

9 × 9	1 × 8	4 × 4	2 × 5	7 × 9	5 × 5	3 × 4	4 × 6	2 × 9	6 × 9
6 × 6	2 × 7	5 × 8	3 × 9	6 × 8	8 × 9	2 × 2	7 × 8	3 × 7	7 × 6
3 × 6	10 × 10	2 × 3	5 × 6	4 × 9	3 × 8	4 × 7	5 × 9	0 × 4	2 × 6
2 × 8	4 × 5	6 × 7	3 × 3	5 × 7	2 × 4	8 × 8	3 × 5	4 × 8	7 × 7

Mental Math

a.	**b.**	**c.**	**d.**
e.	**f.**	**g.**	**h.**

Problem Solving

Understand

What information am I given?

What am I asked to find or do?

- -

Plan

How can I use the information I am given?

Which strategy should I try?

- -

Solve

Did I follow the plan?

Did I show my work?

Did I write the answer?

- -

Check

Did I use the correct information?

Did I do what was asked?

Is my answer reasonable?

Facts   Multiply.

9 × 9	1 × 8	4 × 4	2 × 5	7 × 9	5 × 5	3 × 4	4 × 6	2 × 9	6 × 9
6 × 6	2 × 7	5 × 8	3 × 9	6 × 8	8 × 9	2 × 2	7 × 8	3 × 7	7 × 6
3 × 6	10 × 10	2 × 3	5 × 6	4 × 9	3 × 8	4 × 7	5 × 9	0 × 4	2 × 6
2 × 8	4 × 5	6 × 7	3 × 3	5 × 7	2 × 4	8 × 8	3 × 5	4 × 8	7 × 7

Mental Math

a.	b.	c.	d.
e.	**f.**	**g.**	**h.**

Problem Solving

Understand

What information am I given?
What am I asked to find or do?

- -

Plan

How can I use the information I am given?
Which strategy should I try?

- -

Solve

Did I follow the plan?
Did I show my work?
Did I write the answer?

- -

Check

Did I use the correct information?
Did I do what was asked?
Is my answer reasonable?

Facts   Divide.

9)81	3)27	5)25	2)6	5)45	3)9	4)32	4)16	2)12	7)56
1)9	6)42	2)14	4)28	3)24	5)40	2)18	8)72	3)18	6)54
7)49	2)8	6)36	3)12	8)64	2)4	5)0	4)24	8)8	5)35
3)21	4)20	2)16	5)30	4)36	3)15	6)48	2)10	7)63	8)56

Mental Math

a.	b.	c.	d.
e.	f.	g.	h.

Problem Solving

Understand

What information am I given?
What am I asked to find or do?

Plan

How can I use the information I am given?
Which strategy should I try?

Solve

Did I follow the plan?
Did I show my work?
Did I write the answer?

Check

Did I use the correct information?
Did I do what was asked?
Is my answer reasonable?

Facts   Divide.

9)81	3)27	5)25	2)6	5)45	3)9	4)32	4)16	2)12	7)56
1)9	6)42	2)14	4)28	3)24	5)40	2)18	8)72	3)18	6)54
7)49	2)8	6)36	3)12	8)64	2)4	5)0	4)24	8)8	5)35
3)21	4)20	2)16	5)30	4)36	3)15	6)48	2)10	7)63	8)56

Mental Math

a.	**b.**	**c.**	**d.**
e.	**f.**	**g.**	**h.**

Problem Solving

Understand
What information am I given?
What am I asked to find or do?

Plan
How can I use the information I am given?
Which strategy should I try?

Solve
Did I follow the plan?
Did I show my work?
Did I write the answer?

Check
Did I use the correct information?
Did I do what was asked?
Is my answer reasonable?

Facts Divide.

9)81	3)27	5)25	2)6	5)45	3)9	4)32	4)16	2)12	7)56
1)9	6)42	2)14	4)28	3)24	5)40	2)18	8)72	3)18	6)54
7)49	2)8	6)36	3)12	8)64	2)4	5)0	4)24	8)8	5)35
3)21	4)20	2)16	5)30	4)36	3)15	6)48	2)10	7)63	8)56

Mental Math

a.	b.	c.	d.
e.	f.	g.	h.

Problem Solving

Understand

What information am I given?
What am I asked to find or do?

Plan

How can I use the information I am given?
Which strategy should I try?

Solve

Did I follow the plan?
Did I show my work?
Did I write the answer?

Check

Did I use the correct information?
Did I do what was asked?
Is my answer reasonable?

Facts   Divide.

9⟌81	3⟌27	5⟌25	2⟌6	5⟌45	3⟌9	4⟌32	4⟌16	2⟌12	7⟌56
1⟌9	6⟌42	2⟌14	4⟌28	3⟌24	5⟌40	2⟌18	8⟌72	3⟌18	6⟌54
7⟌49	2⟌8	6⟌36	3⟌12	8⟌64	2⟌4	5⟌0	4⟌24	8⟌8	5⟌35
3⟌21	4⟌20	2⟌16	5⟌30	4⟌36	3⟌15	6⟌48	2⟌10	7⟌63	8⟌56

Mental Math

a.	b.	c.	d.
e.	f.	g.	h.

Problem Solving

Understand
What information am I given?
What am I asked to find or do?

- -

Plan
How can I use the information I am given?
Which strategy should I try?

- -

Solve
Did I follow the plan?
Did I show my work?
Did I write the answer?

- -

Check
Did I use the correct information?
Did I do what was asked?
Is my answer reasonable?

Facts   Multiply.

9 × 9	1 × 8	4 × 4	2 × 5	7 × 9	5 × 5	3 × 4	4 × 6	2 × 9	6 × 9
6 × 6	2 × 7	5 × 8	3 × 9	6 × 8	8 × 9	2 × 2	7 × 8	3 × 7	7 × 6
3 × 6	10 × 10	2 × 3	5 × 6	4 × 9	3 × 8	4 × 7	5 × 9	0 × 4	2 × 6
2 × 8	4 × 5	6 × 7	3 × 3	5 × 7	2 × 4	8 × 8	3 × 5	4 × 8	7 × 7

Mental Math

a.	b.	c.	d.
e.	f.	g.	h.

Problem Solving

Understand

What information am I given?
What am I asked to find or do?

Plan

How can I use the information I am given?
Which strategy should I try?

Solve

Did I follow the plan?
Did I show my work?
Did I write the answer?

Check

Did I use the correct information?
Did I do what was asked?
Is my answer reasonable?

Facts   Multiply.

9 × 9	1 × 8	4 × 4	2 × 5	7 × 9	5 × 5	3 × 4	4 × 6	2 × 9	6 × 9
6 × 6	2 × 7	5 × 8	3 × 9	6 × 8	8 × 9	2 × 2	7 × 8	3 × 7	7 × 6
3 × 6	10 × 10	2 × 3	5 × 6	4 × 9	3 × 8	4 × 7	5 × 9	0 × 4	2 × 6
2 × 8	4 × 5	6 × 7	3 × 3	5 × 7	2 × 4	8 × 8	3 × 5	4 × 8	7 × 7

Mental Math

a.	b.	c.	d.
e.	**f.**	**g.**	**h.**

Problem Solving

Understand

What information am I given?

What am I asked to find or do?

- -

Plan

How can I use the information I am given?

Which strategy should I try?

- -

Solve

Did I follow the plan?

Did I show my work?

Did I write the answer?

- -

Check

Did I use the correct information?

Did I do what was asked?

Is my answer reasonable?

Facts   Multiply.

9 × 9	1 × 8	4 × 4	2 × 5	7 × 9	5 × 5	3 × 4	4 × 6	2 × 9	6 × 9
6 × 6	2 × 7	5 × 8	3 × 9	6 × 8	8 × 9	2 × 2	7 × 8	3 × 7	7 × 6
3 × 6	10 × 10	2 × 3	5 × 6	4 × 9	3 × 8	4 × 7	5 × 9	0 × 4	2 × 6
2 × 8	4 × 5	6 × 7	3 × 3	5 × 7	2 × 4	8 × 8	3 × 5	4 × 8	7 × 7

Mental Math

a.	b.	c.	d.
e.	f.	g.	h.

Problem Solving

Understand

What information am I given?
What am I asked to find or do?

Plan

How can I use the information I am given?
Which strategy should I try?

Solve

Did I follow the plan?
Did I show my work?
Did I write the answer?

Check

Did I use the correct information?
Did I do what was asked?
Is my answer reasonable?

Facts   Multiply.

9 × 9	1 × 8	4 × 4	2 × 5	7 × 9	5 × 5	3 × 4	4 × 6	2 × 9	6 × 9
6 × 6	2 × 7	5 × 8	3 × 9	6 × 8	8 × 9	2 × 2	7 × 8	3 × 7	7 × 6
3 × 6	10 × 10	2 × 3	5 × 6	4 × 9	3 × 8	4 × 7	5 × 9	0 × 4	2 × 6
2 × 8	4 × 5	6 × 7	3 × 3	5 × 7	2 × 4	8 × 8	3 × 5	4 × 8	7 × 7

Mental Math

a.	**b.**	**c.**	**d.**
e.	**f.**	**g.**	**h.**

Problem Solving

Understand
What information am I given?
What am I asked to find or do?

- -

Plan
How can I use the information I am given?
Which strategy should I try?

- -

Solve
Did I follow the plan?
Did I show my work?
Did I write the answer?

- -

Check
Did I use the correct information?
Did I do what was asked?
Is my answer reasonable?

Facts   Multiply.

9 × 9	1 × 8	4 × 4	2 × 5	7 × 9	5 × 5	3 × 4	4 × 6	2 × 9	6 × 9
6 × 6	2 × 7	5 × 8	3 × 9	6 × 8	8 × 9	2 × 2	7 × 8	3 × 7	7 × 6
3 × 6	10 × 10	2 × 3	5 × 6	4 × 9	3 × 8	4 × 7	5 × 9	0 × 4	2 × 6
2 × 8	4 × 5	6 × 7	3 × 3	5 × 7	2 × 4	8 × 8	3 × 5	4 × 8	7 × 7

Mental Math

a.	b.	c.	d.
e.	f.	g.	h.

Problem Solving

Understand

What information am I given?

What am I asked to find or do?

- -

Plan

How can I use the information I am given?

Which strategy should I try?

- -

Solve

Did I follow the plan?

Did I show my work?

Did I write the answer?

- -

Check

Did I use the correct information?

Did I do what was asked?

Is my answer reasonable?

Facts   Divide.

9)81	3)27	5)25	2)6	5)45	3)9	4)32	4)16	2)12	7)56
1)9	6)42	2)14	4)28	3)24	5)40	2)18	8)72	3)18	6)54
7)49	2)8	6)36	3)12	8)64	2)4	5)0	4)24	8)8	5)35
3)21	4)20	2)16	5)30	4)36	3)15	6)48	2)10	7)63	8)56

Mental Math

a.	**b.**	**c.**	**d.**
e.	**f.**	**g.**	**h.**

Problem Solving

Understand

What information am I given?

What am I asked to find or do?

- -

Plan

How can I use the information I am given?

Which strategy should I try?

- -

Solve

Did I follow the plan?

Did I show my work?

Did I write the answer?

- -

Check

Did I use the correct information?

Did I do what was asked?

Is my answer reasonable?

Facts   Divide.

9)81	3)27	5)25	2)6	5)45	3)9	4)32	4)16	2)12	7)56
1)9	6)42	2)14	4)28	3)24	5)40	2)18	8)72	3)18	6)54
7)49	2)8	6)36	3)12	8)64	2)4	5)0	4)24	8)8	5)35
3)21	4)20	2)16	5)30	4)36	3)15	6)48	2)10	7)63	8)56

Mental Math

a.	b.	c.	d.
e.	f.	g.	h.

Problem Solving

Understand
What information am I given?
What am I asked to find or do?

- -

Plan
How can I use the information I am given?
Which strategy should I try?

- -

Solve
Did I follow the plan?
Did I show my work?
Did I write the answer?

- -

Check
Did I use the correct information?
Did I do what was asked?
Is my answer reasonable?

Facts   Divide.

$9\overline{)81}$	$3\overline{)27}$	$5\overline{)25}$	$2\overline{)6}$	$5\overline{)45}$	$3\overline{)9}$	$4\overline{)32}$	$4\overline{)16}$	$2\overline{)12}$	$7\overline{)56}$
$1\overline{)9}$	$6\overline{)42}$	$2\overline{)14}$	$4\overline{)28}$	$3\overline{)24}$	$5\overline{)40}$	$2\overline{)18}$	$8\overline{)72}$	$3\overline{)18}$	$6\overline{)54}$
$7\overline{)49}$	$2\overline{)8}$	$6\overline{)36}$	$3\overline{)12}$	$8\overline{)64}$	$2\overline{)4}$	$5\overline{)0}$	$4\overline{)24}$	$8\overline{)8}$	$5\overline{)35}$
$3\overline{)21}$	$4\overline{)20}$	$2\overline{)16}$	$5\overline{)30}$	$4\overline{)36}$	$3\overline{)15}$	$6\overline{)48}$	$2\overline{)10}$	$7\overline{)63}$	$8\overline{)56}$

Mental Math

a.	**b.**	**c.**	**d.**
e.	**f.**	**g.**	**h.**

Problem Solving

Understand

What information am I given?
What am I asked to find or do?

- -

Plan

How can I use the information I am given?
Which strategy should I try?

- -

Solve

Did I follow the plan?
Did I show my work?
Did I write the answer?

- -

Check

Did I use the correct information?
Did I do what was asked?
Is my answer reasonable?

Facts   Divide.

9)81	3)27	5)25	2)6	5)45	3)9	4)32	4)16	2)12	7)56
1)9	6)42	2)14	4)28	3)24	5)40	2)18	8)72	3)18	6)54
7)49	2)8	6)36	3)12	8)64	2)4	5)0	4)24	8)8	5)35
3)21	4)20	2)16	5)30	4)36	3)15	6)48	2)10	7)63	8)56

Mental Math

a.	**b.**	**c.**	**d.**
e.	**f.**	**g.**	**h.**

Problem Solving

Understand

What information am I given?
What am I asked to find or do?

- -

Plan

How can I use the information I am given?
Which strategy should I try?

- -

Solve

Did I follow the plan?
Did I show my work?
Did I write the answer?

- -

Check

Did I use the correct information?
Did I do what was asked?
Is my answer reasonable?

Facts — Multiply.

8 ×8	0 ×5	7 ×3	9 ×7	3 ×2	9 ×4	8 ×6	4 ×3	9 ×5	6 ×2
9 ×2	7 ×4	8 ×3	5 ×5	9 ×6	7 ×2	5 ×4	9 ×1	9 ×3	0 ×0
7 ×5	2 ×2	6 ×4	8 ×7	5 ×3	7 ×6	4 ×2	8 ×5	6 ×3	9 ×9
3 ×3	8 ×4	7 ×7	8 ×2	10 ×10	6 ×5	4 ×4	9 ×8	5 ×2	6 ×6

Mental Math

a.	**b.**	**c.**	**d.**
e.	**f.**	**g.**	**h.**

Problem Solving

Understand

What information am I given?
What am I asked to find or do?

- -

Plan

How can I use the information I am given?
Which strategy should I try?

- -

Solve

Did I follow the plan?
Did I show my work?
Did I write the answer?

- -

Check

Did I use the correct information?
Did I do what was asked?
Is my answer reasonable?

Facts   Multiply.

8 × 8	0 × 5	7 × 3	9 × 7	3 × 2	9 × 4	8 × 6	4 × 3	9 × 5	6 × 2
9 × 2	7 × 4	8 × 3	5 × 5	9 × 6	7 × 2	5 × 4	9 × 1	9 × 3	0 × 0
7 × 5	2 × 2	6 × 4	8 × 7	5 × 3	7 × 6	4 × 2	8 × 5	6 × 3	9 × 9
3 × 3	8 × 4	7 × 7	8 × 2	10 × 10	6 × 5	4 × 4	9 × 8	5 × 2	6 × 6

Mental Math

a.	**b.**	**c.**	**d.**
e.	**f.**	**g.**	**h.**

Problem Solving

Understand

What information am I given?
What am I asked to find or do?

- -

Plan

How can I use the information I am given?
Which strategy should I try?

- -

Solve

Did I follow the plan?
Did I show my work?
Did I write the answer?

- -

Check

Did I use the correct information?
Did I do what was asked?
Is my answer reasonable?

Facts   Multiply.

8 ×8	0 ×5	7 ×3	9 ×7	3 ×2	9 ×4	8 ×6	4 ×3	9 ×5	6 ×2
9 ×2	7 ×4	8 ×3	5 ×5	9 ×6	7 ×2	5 ×4	9 ×1	9 ×3	0 ×0
7 ×5	2 ×2	6 ×4	8 ×7	5 ×3	7 ×6	4 ×2	8 ×5	6 ×3	9 ×9
3 ×3	8 ×4	7 ×7	8 ×2	10 ×10	6 ×5	4 ×4	9 ×8	5 ×2	6 ×6

Mental Math

a.	b.	c.	d.
e.	**f.**	**g.**	**h.**

Problem Solving

Understand
What information am I given?
What am I asked to find or do?

- -

Plan
How can I use the information I am given?
Which strategy should I try?

- -

Solve
Did I follow the plan?
Did I show my work?
Did I write the answer?

- -

Check
Did I use the correct information?
Did I do what was asked?
Is my answer reasonable?

© Houghton Mifflin Harcourt Publishing Company and Stephen Hake

Facts   Multiply.

8 ×8	0 ×5	7 ×3	9 ×7	3 ×2	9 ×4	8 ×6	4 ×3	9 ×5	6 ×2
9 ×2	7 ×4	8 ×3	5 ×5	9 ×6	7 ×2	5 ×4	9 ×1	9 ×3	0 ×0
7 ×5	2 ×2	6 ×4	8 ×7	5 ×3	7 ×6	4 ×2	8 ×5	6 ×3	9 ×9
3 ×3	8 ×4	7 ×7	8 ×2	10 ×10	6 ×5	4 ×4	9 ×8	5 ×2	6 ×6

Mental Math

a.	**b.**	**c.**	**d.**
e.	**f.**	**g.**	**h.**

Problem Solving

Understand

What information am I given?

What am I asked to find or do?

Plan

How can I use the information I am given?

Which strategy should I try?

Solve

Did I follow the plan?

Did I show my work?

Did I write the answer?

Check

Did I use the correct information?

Did I do what was asked?

Is my answer reasonable?

Facts   Multiply.

8 ×8	0 ×5	7 ×3	9 ×7	3 ×2	9 ×4	8 ×6	4 ×3	9 ×5	6 ×2
9 ×2	7 ×4	8 ×3	5 ×5	9 ×6	7 ×2	5 ×4	9 ×1	9 ×3	0 ×0
7 ×5	2 ×2	6 ×4	8 ×7	5 ×3	7 ×6	4 ×2	8 ×5	6 ×3	9 ×9
3 ×3	8 ×4	7 ×7	8 ×2	10 ×10	6 ×5	4 ×4	9 ×8	5 ×2	6 ×6

Mental Math

a.	**b.**	**c.**	**d.**
e.	**f.**	**g.**	**h.**

Problem Solving

Understand

What information am I given?

What am I asked to find or do?

- -

Plan

How can I use the information I am given?

Which strategy should I try?

- -

Solve

Did I follow the plan?

Did I show my work?

Did I write the answer?

- -

Check

Did I use the correct information?

Did I do what was asked?

Is my answer reasonable?

Facts   Divide.

8)8	6)36	8)16	9)63	8)40	6)12	9)81	5)25	3)9	9)27
8)32	2)4	5)20	9)72	4)12	8)56	8)24	9)36	5)10	9)54
6)18	7)42	3)6	7)35	8)64	4)16	1)7	9)18	6)48	7)28
7)14	3)0	9)45	7)21	6)24	4)8	8)48	6)30	5)15	7)49

Mental Math

a.	b.	c.	d.
e.	f.	g.	h.

Problem Solving

Understand

What information am I given?
What am I asked to find or do?

- -

Plan

How can I use the information I am given?
Which strategy should I try?

- -

Solve

Did I follow the plan?
Did I show my work?
Did I write the answer?

- -

Check

Did I use the correct information?
Did I do what was asked?
Is my answer reasonable?

Facts   Divide.

8)8	6)36	8)16	9)63	8)40	6)12	9)81	5)25	3)9	9)27
8)32	2)4	5)20	9)72	4)12	8)56	8)24	9)36	5)10	9)54
6)18	7)42	3)6	7)35	8)64	4)16	1)7	9)18	6)48	7)28
7)14	3)0	9)45	7)21	6)24	4)8	8)48	6)30	5)15	7)49

Mental Math

a.	**b.**	**c.**	**d.**
e.	**f.**	**g.**	**h.**

Problem Solving

Understand

What information am I given?
What am I asked to find or do?

Plan

How can I use the information I am given?
Which strategy should I try?

Solve

Did I follow the plan?
Did I show my work?
Did I write the answer?

Check

Did I use the correct information?
Did I do what was asked?
Is my answer reasonable?

Facts   Divide.

$8\overline{)8}$	$6\overline{)36}$	$8\overline{)16}$	$9\overline{)63}$	$8\overline{)40}$	$6\overline{)12}$	$9\overline{)81}$	$5\overline{)25}$	$3\overline{)9}$	$9\overline{)27}$
$8\overline{)32}$	$2\overline{)4}$	$5\overline{)20}$	$9\overline{)72}$	$4\overline{)12}$	$8\overline{)56}$	$8\overline{)24}$	$9\overline{)36}$	$5\overline{)10}$	$9\overline{)54}$
$6\overline{)18}$	$7\overline{)42}$	$3\overline{)6}$	$7\overline{)35}$	$8\overline{)64}$	$4\overline{)16}$	$1\overline{)7}$	$9\overline{)18}$	$6\overline{)48}$	$7\overline{)28}$
$7\overline{)14}$	$3\overline{)0}$	$9\overline{)45}$	$7\overline{)21}$	$6\overline{)24}$	$4\overline{)8}$	$8\overline{)48}$	$6\overline{)30}$	$5\overline{)15}$	$7\overline{)49}$

Mental Math

a.	**b.**	**c.**	**d.**
e.	**f.**	**g.**	**h.**

Problem Solving

Understand

What information am I given?
What am I asked to find or do?

- -

Plan

How can I use the information I am given?
Which strategy should I try?

- -

Solve

Did I follow the plan?
Did I show my work?
Did I write the answer?

- -

Check

Did I use the correct information?
Did I do what was asked?
Is my answer reasonable?

Facts — Add.

6 +6	3 +8	5 +9	2 +3	4 +9	3 +4	8 +9	2 +7	0 +3	4 +4
4 +8	2 +9	7 +8	4 +5	9 +1	2 +6	5 +5	6 +7	3 +7	9 +9
7 +9	2 +4	6 +5	3 +3	6 +9	4 +7	0 +0	2 +2	3 +9	5 +8
3 +6	8 +8	4 +6	2 +5	6 +8	3 +5	5 +7	10 +10	2 +8	7 +7

Mental Math

a.	**b.**	**c.**	**d.**
e.	**f.**	**g.**	**h.**

Problem Solving

Understand

What information am I given?
What am I asked to find or do?

- -

Plan

How can I use the information I am given?
Which strategy should I try?

- -

Solve

Did I follow the plan?
Did I show my work?
Did I write the answer?

- -

Check

Did I use the correct information?
Did I do what was asked?
Is my answer reasonable?

| **Facts** | Add. |

6 +6	3 +8	5 +9	2 +3	4 +9	3 +4	8 +9	2 +7	0 +3	4 +4
4 +8	2 +9	7 +8	4 +5	9 +1	2 +6	5 +5	6 +7	3 +7	9 +9
7 +9	2 +4	6 +5	3 +3	6 +9	4 +7	0 +0	2 +2	3 +9	5 +8
3 +6	8 +8	4 +6	2 +5	6 +8	3 +5	5 +7	10 +10	2 +8	7 +7

| **Mental Math** |

a.	b.	c.	d.
e.	f.	g.	h.

| **Problem Solving** |

Understand
What information am I given?
What am I asked to find or do?

Plan
How can I use the information I am given?
Which strategy should I try?

Solve
Did I follow the plan?
Did I show my work?
Did I write the answer?

Check
Did I use the correct information?
Did I do what was asked?
Is my answer reasonable?

Facts Add.

6 +6	3 +8	5 +9	2 +3	4 +9	3 +4	8 +9	2 +7	0 +3	4 +4
4 +8	2 +9	7 +8	4 +5	9 +1	2 +6	5 +5	6 +7	3 +7	9 +9
7 +9	2 +4	6 +5	3 +3	6 +9	4 +7	0 +0	2 +2	3 +9	5 +8
3 +6	8 +8	4 +6	2 +5	6 +8	3 +5	5 +7	10 +10	2 +8	7 +7

Mental Math

a.	**b.**	**c.**	**d.**
e.	**f.**	**g.**	**h.**

Problem Solving

Understand

What information am I given?
What am I asked to find or do?

Plan

How can I use the information I am given?
Which strategy should I try?

Solve

Did I follow the plan?
Did I show my work?
Did I write the answer?

Check

Did I use the correct information?
Did I do what was asked?
Is my answer reasonable?

Facts   Add.

6 +6	3 +8	5 +9	2 +3	4 +9	3 +4	8 +9	2 +7	0 +3	4 +4
4 +8	2 +9	7 +8	4 +5	9 +1	2 +6	5 +5	6 +7	3 +7	9 +9
7 +9	2 +4	6 +5	3 +3	6 +9	4 +7	0 +0	2 +2	3 +9	5 +8
3 +6	8 +8	4 +6	2 +5	6 +8	3 +5	5 +7	10 +10	2 +8	7 +7

Mental Math

a.	b.	c.	d.
e.	f.	g.	h.

Problem Solving

Understand

What information am I given?
What am I asked to find or do?

- -

Plan

How can I use the information I am given?
Which strategy should I try?

- -

Solve

Did I follow the plan?
Did I show my work?
Did I write the answer?

- -

Check

Did I use the correct information?
Did I do what was asked?
Is my answer reasonable?

Facts Add.

6 +6	3 +8	5 +9	2 +3	4 +9	3 +4	8 +9	2 +7	0 +3	4 +4
4 +8	2 +9	7 +8	4 +5	9 +1	2 +6	5 +5	6 +7	3 +7	9 +9
7 +9	2 +4	6 +5	3 +3	6 +9	4 +7	0 +0	2 +2	3 +9	5 +8
3 +6	8 +8	4 +6	2 +5	6 +8	3 +5	5 +7	10 +10	2 +8	7 +7

Mental Math

a.	**b.**	**c.**	**d.**
e.	**f.**	**g.**	**h.**

Problem Solving

Understand

What information am I given?
What am I asked to find or do?

- -

Plan

How can I use the information I am given?
Which strategy should I try?

- -

Solve

Did I follow the plan?
Did I show my work?
Did I write the answer?

- -

Check

Did I use the correct information?
Did I do what was asked?
Is my answer reasonable?

Facts   Subtract.

11 − 9	6 − 0	13 − 6	10 − 3	15 − 7	9 − 6	12 − 9	8 − 2	14 − 7	5 − 3
5 − 2	10 − 8	14 − 6	9 − 4	7 − 5	17 − 8	6 − 3	10 − 5	12 − 6	8 − 3
13 − 4	11 − 6	16 − 8	12 − 7	9 − 5	13 − 5	8 − 4	14 − 5	8 − 8	9 − 7
15 − 6	6 − 2	10 − 4	17 − 9	16 − 7	7 − 4	12 − 8	4 − 2	18 − 9	11 − 8

Mental Math

a.	**b.**	**c.**	**d.**
e.	**f.**	**g.**	**h.**

Problem Solving

Understand

What information am I given?
What am I asked to find or do?

- -

Plan

How can I use the information I am given?
Which strategy should I try?

- -

Solve

Did I follow the plan?
Did I show my work?
Did I write the answer?

- -

Check

Did I use the correct information?
Did I do what was asked?
Is my answer reasonable?

Facts Multiply.

8 × 7	6 × 3	8 × 4	8 × 3	8 × 6
4 × 3	7 × 4	7 × 3	7 × 6	6 × 4
3 × 7	4 × 6	4 × 8	6 × 8	3 × 4
6 × 7	7 × 8	3 × 6	3 × 8	4 × 7

Mental Math

a.	**b.**	**c.**	**d.**
e.	**f.**	**g.**	**h.**

Problem Solving

Understand

What information am I given?
What am I asked to find or do?

- -

Plan

How can I use the information I am given?
Which strategy should I try?

- -

Solve

Did I follow the plan?
Did I show my work?
Did I write the answer?

- -

Check

Did I use the correct information?
Did I do what was asked?
Is my answer reasonable?

Facts — Subtract.

11 −9	6 −0	13 −6	10 −3	15 −7	9 −6	12 −9	8 −2	14 −7	5 −3
5 −2	10 −8	14 −6	9 −4	7 −5	17 −8	6 −3	10 −5	12 −6	8 −3
13 −4	11 −6	16 −8	12 −7	9 −5	13 −5	8 −4	14 −5	8 −8	9 −7
15 −6	6 −2	10 −4	17 −9	16 −7	7 −4	12 −8	4 −2	18 −9	11 −8

Mental Math

a.	b.	c.	d.
e.	f.	g.	h.

Problem Solving

Understand
What information am I given?
What am I asked to find or do?

Plan
How can I use the information I am given?
Which strategy should I try?

Solve
Did I follow the plan?
Did I show my work?
Did I write the answer?

Check
Did I use the correct information?
Did I do what was asked?
Is my answer reasonable?

Facts   Subtract.

11 −9	6 −0	13 −6	10 −3	15 −7	9 −6	12 −9	8 −2	14 −7	5 −3
5 −2	10 −8	14 −6	9 −4	7 −5	17 −8	6 −3	10 −5	12 −6	8 −3
13 −4	11 −6	16 −8	12 −7	9 −5	13 −5	8 −4	14 −5	8 −8	9 −7
15 −6	6 −2	10 −4	17 −9	16 −7	7 −4	12 −8	4 −2	18 −9	11 −8

Mental Math

a.	b.	c.	d.
e.	f.	g.	h.

Problem Solving

Understand

What information am I given?
What am I asked to find or do?

- -

Plan

How can I use the information I am given?
Which strategy should I try?

- -

Solve

Did I follow the plan?
Did I show my work?
Did I write the answer?

- -

Check

Did I use the correct information?
Did I do what was asked?
Is my answer reasonable?

Facts   Multiply.

5 ×5	1 ×8	0 ×6	9 ×2	5 ×4	1 ×1	2 ×3	5 ×3	3 ×0	1 ×9
9 ×0	8 ×5	1 ×5	6 ×5	1 ×0	4 ×2	4 ×5	7 ×0	2 ×7	6 ×1
6 ×2	5 ×0	2 ×2	1 ×3	5 ×6	5 ×7	0 ×0	8 ×2	9 ×5	4 ×1
2 ×1	5 ×8	0 ×2	3 ×5	5 ×9	8 ×0	1 ×7	2 ×5	0 ×4	7 ×5

Mental Math

a.	**b.**	**c.**	**d.**
e.	**f.**	**g.**	**h.**

Problem Solving

Understand
What information am I given?
What am I asked to find or do?

Plan
How can I use the information I am given?
Which strategy should I try?

Solve
Did I follow the plan?
Did I show my work?
Did I write the answer?

Check
Did I use the correct information?
Did I do what was asked?
Is my answer reasonable?

Facts   Multiply.

9 × 9	1 × 8	4 × 4	2 × 5	7 × 9	5 × 5	3 × 4	4 × 6	2 × 9	6 × 9
6 × 6	2 × 7	5 × 8	3 × 9	6 × 8	8 × 9	2 × 2	7 × 8	3 × 7	7 × 6
3 × 6	10 × 10	2 × 3	5 × 6	4 × 9	3 × 8	4 × 7	5 × 9	0 × 4	2 × 6
2 × 8	4 × 5	6 × 7	3 × 3	5 × 7	2 × 4	8 × 8	3 × 5	4 × 8	7 × 7

Mental Math

a.	b.	c.	d.
e.	**f.**	**g.**	**h.**

Problem Solving

Understand

What information am I given?
What am I asked to find or do?

- -

Plan

How can I use the information I am given?
Which strategy should I try?

- -

Solve

Did I follow the plan?
Did I show my work?
Did I write the answer?

- -

Check

Did I use the correct information?
Did I do what was asked?
Is my answer reasonable?

Facts   Divide.

9)81	3)27	5)25	2)6	5)45	3)9	4)32	4)16	2)12	7)56
1)9	6)42	2)14	4)28	3)24	5)40	2)18	8)72	3)18	6)54
7)49	2)8	6)36	3)12	8)64	2)4	5)0	4)24	8)8	5)35
3)21	4)20	2)16	5)30	4)36	3)15	6)48	2)10	7)63	8)56

Mental Math

a.	b.	c.	d.
e.	f.	g.	h.

Problem Solving

Understand
What information am I given?
What am I asked to find or do?

Plan
How can I use the information I am given?
Which strategy should I try?

Solve
Did I follow the plan?
Did I show my work?
Did I write the answer?

Check
Did I use the correct information?
Did I do what was asked?
Is my answer reasonable?

Facts   Multiply.

8 ×8	0 ×5	7 ×3	9 ×7	3 ×2	9 ×4	8 ×6	4 ×3	9 ×5	6 ×2
9 ×2	7 ×4	8 ×3	5 ×5	9 ×6	7 ×2	5 ×4	9 ×1	9 ×3	0 ×0
7 ×5	2 ×2	6 ×4	8 ×7	5 ×3	7 ×6	4 ×2	8 ×5	6 ×3	9 ×9
3 ×3	8 ×4	7 ×7	8 ×2	10 ×10	6 ×5	4 ×4	9 ×8	5 ×2	6 ×6

Mental Math

a.	b.	c.	d.
e.	**f.**	**g.**	**h.**

Problem Solving

Understand

What information am I given?
What am I asked to find or do?

- -

Plan

How can I use the information I am given?
Which strategy should I try?

- -

Solve

Did I follow the plan?
Did I show my work?
Did I write the answer?

- -

Check

Did I use the correct information?
Did I do what was asked?
Is my answer reasonable?

Facts   Multiply.

8 ×8	0 ×5	7 ×3	9 ×7	3 ×2	9 ×4	8 ×6	4 ×3	9 ×5	6 ×2
9 ×2	7 ×4	8 ×3	5 ×5	9 ×6	7 ×2	5 ×4	9 ×1	9 ×3	0 ×0
7 ×5	2 ×2	6 ×4	8 ×7	5 ×3	7 ×6	4 ×2	8 ×5	6 ×3	9 ×9
3 ×3	8 ×4	7 ×7	8 ×2	10 ×10	6 ×5	4 ×4	9 ×8	5 ×2	6 ×6

Mental Math

a.	**b.**	**c.**	**d.**
e.	**f.**	**g.**	**h.**

Problem Solving

Understand

What information am I given?

What am I asked to find or do?

- -

Plan

How can I use the information I am given?

Which strategy should I try?

- -

Solve

Did I follow the plan?

Did I show my work?

Did I write the answer?

- -

Check

Did I use the correct information?

Did I do what was asked?

Is my answer reasonable?

Facts   Multiply.

8 × 8	0 × 5	7 × 3	9 × 7	3 × 2	9 × 4	8 × 6	4 × 3	9 × 5	6 × 2
9 × 2	7 × 4	8 × 3	5 × 5	9 × 6	7 × 2	5 × 4	9 × 1	9 × 3	0 × 0
7 × 5	2 × 2	6 × 4	8 × 7	5 × 3	7 × 6	4 × 2	8 × 5	6 × 3	9 × 9
3 × 3	8 × 4	7 × 7	8 × 2	10 × 10	6 × 5	4 × 4	9 × 8	5 × 2	6 × 6

Mental Math

a.	b.	c.	d.
e.	f.	g.	h.

Problem Solving

Understand
What information am I given?
What am I asked to find or do?

- -

Plan
How can I use the information I am given?
Which strategy should I try?

- -

Solve
Did I follow the plan?
Did I show my work?
Did I write the answer?

- -

Check
Did I use the correct information?
Did I do what was asked?
Is my answer reasonable?

Facts   Divide.

8)8	6)36	8)16	9)63	8)40	6)12	9)81	5)25	3)9	9)27
8)32	2)4	5)20	9)72	4)12	8)56	8)24	9)36	5)10	9)54
6)18	7)42	3)6	7)35	8)64	4)16	1)7	9)18	6)48	7)28
7)14	3)0	9)45	7)21	6)24	4)8	8)48	6)30	5)15	7)49

Mental Math

a.	b.	c.	d.
e.	f.	g.	h.

Problem Solving

Understand

What information am I given?

What am I asked to find or do?

- -

Plan

How can I use the information I am given?

Which strategy should I try?

- -

Solve

Did I follow the plan?

Did I show my work?

Did I write the answer?

- -

Check

Did I use the correct information?

Did I do what was asked?

Is my answer reasonable?

Facts   Divide.

9)81	3)27	5)25	2)6	5)45	3)9	4)32	4)16	2)12	7)56
1)9	6)42	2)14	4)28	3)24	5)40	2)18	8)72	3)18	6)54
7)49	2)8	6)36	3)12	8)64	2)4	5)0	4)24	8)8	5)35
3)21	4)20	2)16	5)30	4)36	3)15	6)48	2)10	7)63	8)56

Mental Math

a.	b.	c.	d.
e.	f.	g.	h.

Problem Solving

Understand

What information am I given?

What am I asked to find or do?

Plan

How can I use the information I am given?

Which strategy should I try?

Solve

Did I follow the plan?

Did I show my work?

Did I write the answer?

Check

Did I use the correct information?

Did I do what was asked?

Is my answer reasonable?

Facts   Divide.

$8\overline{)8}$	$6\overline{)36}$	$8\overline{)16}$	$9\overline{)63}$	$8\overline{)40}$	$6\overline{)12}$	$9\overline{)81}$	$5\overline{)25}$	$3\overline{)9}$	$9\overline{)27}$
$8\overline{)32}$	$2\overline{)4}$	$5\overline{)20}$	$9\overline{)72}$	$4\overline{)12}$	$8\overline{)56}$	$8\overline{)24}$	$9\overline{)36}$	$5\overline{)10}$	$9\overline{)54}$
$6\overline{)18}$	$7\overline{)42}$	$3\overline{)6}$	$7\overline{)35}$	$8\overline{)64}$	$4\overline{)16}$	$1\overline{)7}$	$9\overline{)18}$	$6\overline{)48}$	$7\overline{)28}$
$7\overline{)14}$	$3\overline{)0}$	$9\overline{)45}$	$7\overline{)21}$	$6\overline{)24}$	$4\overline{)8}$	$8\overline{)48}$	$6\overline{)30}$	$5\overline{)15}$	$7\overline{)49}$

Mental Math

a.	**b.**	**c.**	**d.**
e.	**f.**	**g.**	**h.**

Problem Solving

Understand
What information am I given?
What am I asked to find or do?

- -

Plan
How can I use the information I am given?
Which strategy should I try?

- -

Solve
Did I follow the plan?
Did I show my work?
Did I write the answer?

- -

Check
Did I use the correct information?
Did I do what was asked?
Is my answer reasonable?

Facts   Divide.

8)8	6)36	8)16	9)63	8)40	6)12	9)81	5)25	3)9	9)27
8)32	2)4	5)20	9)72	4)12	8)56	8)24	9)36	5)10	9)54
6)18	7)42	3)6	7)35	8)64	4)16	1)7	9)18	6)48	7)28
7)14	3)0	9)45	7)21	6)24	4)8	8)48	6)30	5)15	7)49

Mental Math

a.	b.	c.	d.
e.	f.	g.	h.

Problem Solving

Understand
What information am I given?
What am I asked to find or do?

- -

Plan
How can I use the information I am given?
Which strategy should I try?

- -

Solve
Did I follow the plan?
Did I show my work?
Did I write the answer?

- -

Check
Did I use the correct information?
Did I do what was asked?
Is my answer reasonable?